Crosscurrents / Modern Critiques
Third Series
Edited by Jerome Klinkowitz

Ihab Hassan

OUT OF EGYPT
Scenes and Arguments of
an Autobiography

Southern Illinois University Press
CARBONDALE AND EDWARDSVILLE

Printed in the United States of America

Edited by Curtis L. Clark
Designed by Design for Publishing, Inc.

Library of Congress Cataloging-in-Publication Data

Hassan, Ihab Habib, 1925–
    Out of Egypt.

    (Crosscurrents/modern critiques. Third series)
    1. Hassan, Ihab Habib, 1925–   . 2. Critics—
United States—Biography. 3. Critics—Egypt—Biography.
I. Title.
PN75.H34A36   1986   809 [B]   85–30379
ISBN 0-8093-1296-4

Contents

Foreword

From the crosscurrents of developing culture emerge patterns whose significance will be unquestioned many ages hence. The experiments of one generation are canonized by the next, as lower-case speculations are capitalized by succeeding self-interests. Cultural discourse is an evolving organism, with the only constant being change—"a tradition of the new," as Harold Rosenberg called it, the result of that famous modern break with tradition now having lasted long enough to produce a tradition of its own.

Forging an appropriate role for the critic in such circumstances is the task to which Ihab Hassan dedicates himself. For him, the critic is far more than a conservator and maker of judgments. A critic's duties are as large as the subject he or she comprehends, and from the start Hassan's vision has been broadly extensive. "The contemporary American novel does not only aver our presence," he announces in his first work, *Radical Innocence* (Princeton University Press, 1961), "it explores and enlarges the modalities of our *being*." With the modern soul poised on the eve of Creation, he cautions that "this is not a time for professors of literature to ignore the judgment of human passions," and in his own work proceeds to investigate not just the state of current literature but the deepest thoughts and feelings which inform it. "The important questions before the human race are not literary questions," he acknowledges in *Paracriticisms* (University of Illinois Press, 1975). "They are questions of consciousness—reason, dream, love."

These questions have led Hassan to explore the consequences of outrage and apocalypse in *The Literature of Silence* (Knopf, 1967), "a work of testimony and personal criticism," and to ask the radical questions which "engage the totality of our life" in *The Dismemberment of Orpheus* (Oxford University Press, 1971). In this latter work Hassan discovers his most important theme, that the "imagination may yet prove to be the teleological organ of evolution." *The Right Promethean Fire* (University of Illinois Press, 1980), which considers imagination, science, and cultural change, is dedicated to this proposition.

It is also "the fragment of an imaginary autobiography," and thus leads directly to the work at hand. From Henry Miller, Hassan has learned that "writing is autobiography, and autobiography is therapy, which is a form of action on the self." As Paul Valéry teaches: "there is no theory that is not a fragment, carefully concealed, of some autobiography." If indeed humankind is being transformed by a new universal consciousness of mind, as Hassan's work progressively suggests, it is right that critics address their own evolution as thinking and feeling beings.

Ihab Hassan's vision as critic and cultural spokesperson has been creatively visionary, providing an important beacon for the Crosscurrents project as it expresses contemporary critical thought. "Whoever undertakes to create," Harold Rosenberg counseled, "soon finds himself engaged in creating himself," and it is in the proper transitive reading of this latter phrase—of self-creation—that Ihab Hassan's *Out of Egypt* is understood.

Jerome Klinkowitz

Preface

Prefaces cast certain shadows on themselves. The preface to an autobiography may be shadier still: it seeks to justify what is already justification. In brevity, then, we may chance on clarity.

My story began in Egypt, continues in America. But how tell that story of disjunction, self-exile? In fragments, I think, in slips of memory, scraps of thought. In scenes and arguments of a life time, re-membered like the scattered bones of Osiris.

As it happened, I wrote this book in Munich and Milwaukee. These two—I nearly said twin—cities ground the narrative in the bland present, from which errant memory constantly departs, only to return again. These cities provide the "scene of writing," where life, language, and reflection run their current course. They, too, are part of the story.

Scholar, critic, teacher, I have spent some part of my life in thought. Thus story and meditation mingle in this work, rumor, rumination, and recall. Nor is it easy, in our present world, to see where history begins, autobiography ends. Cracks run through both, run through all contemporary existence, a fractious existence, full of silence and fury, seduction and terror. I have interjected in my narrative brief essays—one page, two pages long—as if to fill these cracks.

The reader may encounter here other distractions: quotations, brief interludes. In this time of immanent media, minds blend into minds, voices into voices. This is the burden of our intertextual, our gnostic, age. But some quotations here come from my own previous work. Call it self-plagiarism or self-anthologizing; these citations still refract thoughts, moments, from another day. Refractions and breaks: yes, they hinder the superficial flow. But deeper, perhaps, the reader may discover a coherence of motive, a tighter tale similar to his or her own. There is more than one way of reading, which each reader will know. Good reader, skip or find your pace. The last brief chapter, in any case, attempts to gather beginnings and ends into its middle, with fewer hindrances to the eye. But it cannot, of course, complete the story.

One last word about veracity, the truth of the page. This work is not an "imaginary autobiography," though it takes some slight liberty with a few scenes and names. But "veracity"? I know something of the cunning of desire, duplicity of memoration. Against these, we can only summon the will to authenticity, in mutual trust.

Acknowledgments

The first chapter of this work appeared, rather differently, in the *Kenyon Review* (Summer 1983) and the second appeared, in an earlier, shorter form, in *SubStance* 37/38 (Winter-Spring 1983).

My appreciation endures for the University of Wisconsin–Milwaukee and for the Vilas Trust Estate: their support has made this, as earlier, writing an integral part of my work. Wolfgang and Thérèse Ule helped me to revisit Egypt in memory, their own memories of the place perhaps kindlier than mine. A few friends—Matei Calinescu, Richard Martin, Earl Rovit—commented acutely on the manuscript. Walter Abish offered encouragement and advised me with genial and preternatural insight on central issues of the book. I am grateful to them all.

It was my wife, Sally Hassan, though, who prompted me to overcome, at last, my reluctance to write my past. She inspired this work—in which she is both absent and present—as she remains the unique presence of my life.

Out of Egypt

Scenes and Arguments of an Autobiography

[Criticism] is the only civilized form of autobiography, as it deals not with events, but with the thoughts of one's life; not with life's physical accidents of deed and circumstance, but with the spiritual moods and imaginative passions of the need.

Oscar Wilde
Intentions

———◆———

Of late, I have come to sense within myself an accumulation of all kinds of things that cannot find adequate expression via an objective artistic form such as the novel. A lyric poet of twenty might manage it, but I am twenty no longer, and have never been a poet at any rate. I have groped around, therefore, for some other form more suited to such personal utterances and have come up with a kind of hybrid between confession and criticism, a subtly equivocal mode that one might call "confidential criticism."

Yukio Mishima
Sun and Steel

———◆———

He who has once begun to open the fan of memory never comes to the end of its segments; no image satisfies him, for he has seen that it can be unfolded, and only in its folds does the truth reside.

Walter Benjamin
Reflections

1

Beginnings and Ends

ON A BURNING AUGUST afternoon in 1946, brisk wind and salt of the Mediterranean on my lips, I boarded the *Abraham Lincoln* at Port Said and sailed from Egypt, never to return. My father gave me a gold Movado wristwatch, and waved me goodbye from a bobbing white launch. I waved back, not daring to shout or speak. Churning tugs nosed the battered Liberty Ship into the seaways. I saw the town, the minarets, the high cupola of the Compagnie de Suez, recede. I saw the sands of Sinai shimmer, fade. And gliding past the great bronze statue of Ferdinand de Lesseps, who rose from the barnacled jetty above breaker and spume, one hand pointing imperiously east, I could only think: "I did it! I did it! I'm bound for New York!"

Thus began my passage to America. New birth or false rebirth? I had not heard yet of Whitman—"Passage indeed, O soul, to primal thought!"—nor read much about Columbus.

Here I must set down beginnings, themes, ends.
I was born on 17 October 1925, in Cairo, Egypt, and
though I carry papers that solemnly record this date
and place, I have never felt these facts decisive in my
life. I do not recall the house I was born in. Years later,
driving by in our silver Packard, my grandmother would
point out the house to me, still standing, tall and glum,
in the now rowdy heart of the city. Its grill, its narrow
doors and blank shutters, seemed always closed against
my gaze as if holding some riddle.

The Sphinx, *Abu²l Hol* (Father of Terror) himself,
crouched but a few leagues away, as Egyptian crows fly,
in its sandy hollow at Giza. Huge, pocked face, nose
chipped, wild eyes staring in the wind. Still, the thing
inspired no fear in me, nor stirred ancestral memories.
Behind it rose that abstract wonder of the Seven Wonders, the Great Pyramid, transcendent will in desert
landscape. Seen with boyish eyes, it offered no promise
except that I might some day clamber up its jagged edge
and so claim an end to my puberty. Yet there were a few
times when, its vermillion image glistening in newly-
watered fields, it suddenly dissolved in the mind as if
stone could become quintessence of thought.

"17 October 1925, Cairo, Egypt": strange, stubborn
ciphers to conjure time and space, and appease mortality, our mystery.

◆

INTERLUDE

In his *Letters from Egypt*, Gustave Flaubert writes about
the Great Pyramid *before* ever seeing it: "Look! Lend an
ear, listen and look O traveler! O thinker! And your

thirst will be appeased, and all your life will have passed like a dream, for you will feel your soul go out toward the light and soar in the infinite."

Is this luminous nonsense or genuine fancy at play? Having seen the pyramids a thousand times in my childhood, I may still write about them now, like Flaubert, as if I never had. For all autobiography is myth, like Death itself, in its deepest reality imaginary.

Like other Egyptian children, I walked among the ancient gods unseeing. Amon, Horus, Set, Hathor, Nu, Mut, Khnum, Anubis, Isis, Osiris: they all haunt the world's museums. In our house they lived only as carvings on lacquered chairs, replicas of Pharaonic thrones awkward to sit on. By their side, Turkish hassocks, Arabesque tables, copper trays engraved intricately with the Koran, and European art nouveau furnishings cluttered my imaginary space. The old gods with animal heads could still evoke a childish shudder in a room darkened against the midday sun. But their awful power, like much else in Egypt, had long fled.

My childhood space: it was indeed a palimpsest of styles, babel of tongues. French and Arabic were my first languages; but I liked far more another which I now write; and I speak all with a slight foreign sound. Who reckons the deep declensions of Desire, inflections of the Logos, or denials of a Mother's Tongue? Does "matricide" free men into alien speech?

Egypt herself is a palimpsest of cultures, her history an echolalia of conquering tongues, so greedy everyone seems to have been of this slender, green Bride of the Nile. Hyksos shepherds first came on their horses and also Libyan desert nomads; then fighting Assyrians, followed by mad Medes; Greeks and Romans invaded next, bringing Christianity in their wake; Arabs swooped down on the edge of their faith and scimitars, leaving behind the enduring culture of Islam; Mamelukes and Turks brought only their gruesome ways, till Napoleon, *Sultan El Kebir,* drove them out and so "restored Egypt to the world." But the French stayed only till Nelson defeated their fleet at Abukir; the British felt then duty bound to hold Egypt in their trust until 1954.

Thus, more conquered than conquering since Ramses the Second, Egypt became less bride to nature than crossroads to history. Yet it preserves a peerless continuity of five millennia, a continuity of estival rhythms and human miseries. For Egypt endures as the *fellah* endures, breeding and dying in the rich loam of the Nile, following his beast around the pound as the *sakiah* trickles water into fecund fields. Do his roots reach back to incestuous Pharaohs and animal gods? And what avail those roots, sick as he is and starving in the shadow of a history more pitiless than the sun?

Roots, everyone speaks of roots. I have cared for none. Perhaps, in my case, they were too old and tangled; or perhaps they withered early from some blight, which I have long ceased to mourn. Looking as a child upon those ancestors chiseled in stone, so rigid in posture yet so fluid in line, ancestors who stared eternity down and answered to uncouth names, I bore away no kinship feelings. Still, who knows but that their Ka, uniting Life and Death in its Essential Self, did not inscribe some hieratic message in my soul?

MUNICH

1981: my wife, Sally, and I have chosen to spend a sabbatical term in Munich. Here I commence to write this book. But Tutankhamun has just invaded the city. As in Paris, London, Toronto, Moscow, and New York, the boy king conquers wherever he goes, from across the grave.

"I see wonderful things," Howard Carter whispered in 1932 to Lord Carnarvon from the depths of King Tut's tomb in Thebes, surrounded by the gold and silence of three thousand and three hundred years. But what do all these eyes now swarming around the luminous glass cases—neatly numbered from "1. Selket" to "55. *Goldene Schlange*"—really see? I find myself looking not at exquisite artifices but at wondering German eyes in a golden glow. And suddenly I recall two other pairs of eyes I once saw.

The first was in an Egyptian mummy's mask, eyes thickly *kohled* around the rims, staring serenely into time, yet with just that shade of doubt, flicker of mortality, to tease death into thought.

The other was in an archaic Grecian head, smiling with ineffable astonishment—amazement and amusement blending there that life should prove to be just so!—having recently awoken from aeons of material sleep.

And I wondered there and then—on this "sabbatical to write a book about the humanities" that turned out to be more a book about myself—I wondered if all that we care to know about ourselves may not lie between

those two immemorial gazes, more than in Tutankhamun's impassive golden face or the Sphinx's nefarious
jest.

———◆———

Growing up in Egypt.
I stand before my uncle, Hafez Pacha Hassan, who
frowns at me from his ogre's height. His white mustache
twitches thinly over his lips.
"And what will you be when you grow up?"
"A warrior, a warrior," I cry, "better than Alexander
or Thutmose the Third."
"A general?" he asks.
"And also a saint."
Faint smiles as I rush out of the room with hot cheeks.
Barely five years old, I suffered already from an implacable shyness. More than others—or so I thought—
I dreaded humiliation, and both dread and pride conspired in my need for self-creation, perpetual re-creation.
Self-recreation: a sovereign fiction that yet enabled
me to resist, even to remake, "things as they are." It
helped me slip through my birthrights: language and
the clutching blood. Slip? We tear ourselves free. We
learn murder in the family, as the ancient Greeks knew,
and rehearse the pride of Oedipus before the Sphinx.
With luck, courage, grace, we may shed our violence at
last and, like ancient heroes, rise to myth.
But how many of us are truly transfigured in myth?
I carry childhood memories of a different kind, lapsed
terrors, strange only to those, like myself, who recall few
dreams:
—my bedroom air shredding in the night as my par-

ents, returning from some white-tie gala, slash one another in the hall with words I cannot yet understand . . .

—a gap-toothed English governness wrapping me up in some henna-colored cotton roll, saturated with iodine, meant to drive out a cold, setting my skin on fire . . .

—a monster Red Sea lobster, the first I had seen of its kind, drowning into our sweet-water garden fountain, all lashing tail and snapping claws, exhaling nightmares in the sun . . .

—a smiling orderly with mustache waxed straight up, his brass-buckled belt creaking in one hand as with the other he leads a servant girl to the basement, from which her shrieks rise, rise . . .

—my father ordering the driver suddenly to stop on a deserted road, getting out to stretch on his back full length in the dust, eyes riveted blankly to the sky . . .

This, too, is Egypt, memories quickened by aging desire, a slow land corruptly dreaming.

ON IDEOLOGY

Small nightmares bind us each to each. Though wise men say experience begins bitterly, bruising bone and gnawing the marrow of the self, I recall little bitterness in my life, and recall even less remorse. And so I am nettled by ideological beings, men and women perpetually aggrieved before existence, who hope to find in some sullen dogma surcease from their sorrow or complaint. Does justice, as Nietzsche thought, always begin in spite and end only when vengeance has drunk its fill? Perhaps this is our common fate. Born terribly unequal—for nature seems too generous to be just, her happier mutations the only grace we can expect—we die with the inequity and iniquity of death on our lips. And what nature fails to skew at birth, culture may thwart later in life, though culture was meant to set things right. And so we hobble on our ideological crutches, pausing to pick up scraps of self-esteem along the way.

I have said: "I can recall little bitterness in my life, and recall even less remorse." Does the statement disguise dire evasions? Perhaps psychoanalysts can tell—I have not sought their help. In any case, as an only child, I felt inward with solitude, and saw less of my parents than of nurses, tutors, domestics, chattering in different tongues. And like many a child, I waited in my small agony for Father and Mother to go out of the house in order to breathe the air of make-believe.

Yet my family teemed with uncles, aunts, cousins. Feckless, greedy, intemperate, spendthrift often and rarely wise, my family was insufferable as all families must seem to those born to reclusion or exile. Certain incidents, moments, quiddities of their lives flash through my mind:

—A paternal uncle. A minister of interior with a gleaming golden tooth, he once forced his cook to swallow scalding bean soup before twelve astonished guests to whom the soup was untimely served.

—A paternal aunt. Assigned to oblivion because she "married beneath her," she remained unknown to me till I was fifty-five. On her deathbed, she wrote to me, through a lawyer, a letter that may have been composed by some Venusian, so little there could I understand.

—A maternal uncle. Inspired, impatient, occasionally mad, he gambled obsessively and finally died by his own hand. Once he ran naked through the house, pursued by his wife, straw-colored tresses streaming and kitchen knife in hand, who kept screaming: "He lost again! I'll cut off *betao* (his thing), I will!"

—Another maternal uncle. He married a raven-haired movie star (honey flowed in her voice, love danced in her liquid eyes). After borrowing a fortune to produce an "epic" on the expulsion of the Medes from Egypt, he found his film confiscated before its release: the Shah of Shahs, descendant of the Medes, had just married King Farouk's sister.

—Still another maternal uncle. First born and the apple of his mother's eyes, he was the first Egyptian judge to sit on that vestige of colonialism, the Supreme Mixed Court for aliens. Like Solomon, he adjudicated my childhood squabbles with his children, playmates in contentious paradise. He was struck by some mysterious sleeping disease, and later found to have embezzled the entire family estate.

—A paternal cousin. He studied engineering in Switzerland, and rowed to a scull championship on the Zürichsee. I never saw him but laughing. When he died at twenty-five—no one knew or told how—his father stopped speaking altogether.

—A maternal granduncle. He sculpted in granite the emblem of *Egypt Renascent,* which stood in front of Cairo's main Railway Station till car fumes sculpted

his sculpture away. He, too, I heard in whispers, became insane, ended a suicide. Or did I hear the whispers of mythomanes?

—My maternal grandmother. She was ample, illiter-
ate, and sage. I learned from her to enjoy food—
pigeons baked in milk and rice—play backgammon,
and hear the unsaid in every speech. She hounded
me to take her to Hollywood movies, and, cocking an
ear, would become cross if I translated too little or too
late. Next to supervising family repasts, she liked best
to see the world go by from her veranda, her foot
tapping on a frayed velvet stool to an inaudible rhythm
of things.

—My "other grandmother." Not a grandmother at all
but my wet nurse, a Greek called Helena, she kept
reappearing throughout my early years, protective,
slate-gray eyes unsmiling. She seemed rock-like, ele-
mental, a sculpture by Maillol, a Henry Moore without
loopholes. Before her force, Egyptian levity receded, so
much froth. She spoke to me sometimes of her old home
in Constantinople, and of Hagia Sophia, which became
under my ancestors, the Turks, a great mosque. When I
visited Istanbul half a century later, I saw the place, a
desacralized space, now museum, the perfect dome
and arches still carrying Sophia's mystic wisdom beneath layers of alien splendor. And I thought of Helena, of Greeks and Turks, of blood spent and begotten,
and blood mixed in forgotten ravishments. Was she,
of the capable breasts, my other grandmother after
all?

And my parents, my own parents? Who will recall
them now, if not I, their sole son? Who will speak them?
In their case, I do not know—*will* not know?—whereof

I speak. Whatever passions or pains speed our childish days, we grow up to become familial ghosts, eidolons signaling to one another across darkening inscapes of memory. "Where" are my parents, now dead, where anyone, including Thutmose the Third and great Ramses, except in the shadow world of representations? Only language, simulacrum of our presence, speaks.

But really: *only* language speaks? I have never quite believed it.

MUNICH

My twenty-four-year-old son has come to visit us in Munich. He asks incredulously: "Dad, you're writing an autobiography? But you never spoke of Egypt at home!"

Geoffrey has been to Egypt twice, on short trips with his mother, Bolly, my first wife. He has seen my parents in the late evening of their lives. (I last saw them in Geneva, in 1963, more than a decade earlier.) What does he remember of Egypt, of his grandparents? Everything. But he chooses to yield only a few images at a time.

He remembers his grandmother, always peremptory till she began to lose her memory after her husband's death, two years before her own. Once, Geoffrey recalls, in the restaurant of the new Shepheard's Hotel, she held her handbag at arm's length till a bus boy came running with an extra chair to put it on. She did not look at him.

Later, she kept a suitcase fully packed under her bed. She spoke rarely, and only of the absent. The snapshots Geoffrey took of her show a slightly hunched figure, determined, a lined face congealed in an expression of permanent pain and disgust.

He has brought the snapshots to Munich—to remind me of my own parents?

———————◆———————

I have said: "Of my parents, I do not know how to speak." Such tergiversations preserve our self-ignorance even as they enhance our self-esteem. Compounding evasions, I could add that I do not know how to "speak Egypt" any more. For I was even there, even then, a stranger: in my native land young beggars on the Cairo streets followed me crying, "*Baksheesh, ya khawaga* (Mr. Foreigner), *baksheesh.*" Writing so many years later, I realize how much of "my Egypt" has vanished, available neither to history nor legend, only to dubious, private recall.

Cairo has drastically changed in half a century, more than Paris, London, or New York. When I attended the Saidiah Secondary School, the city counted less than two million inhabitants; now it pullulates with six or seven times that number. Or is it really more, with numberless peasants dying in the dusty streets which serve them as home? Telephones worked perfectly then, though Egyptians tended instinctively to shout over trunk calls to overwhelm longer distances. My schoolmates and I argued endlessly over *el telephone* about our homework, not about sports or dates, known to us only as the fruit of palm. Traffic jams were unfamiliar to us—jams abounded only on breakfast tables. Streetcars were fun to ride, clanging and careening as they hurtled by on rails; and though most passengers rode hanging from a leather strap or perched zanily on side boards, others, who could afford a few more piasters, found a place in the straw-cushioned compartments marked "First Class Only."

Egyptian bureaucracy was tangled then; now it has become miasmic, I hear. King Fuad, succeeded by King Farouk, still reigned, though "reigning" fails to describe the obese and obscene presence of the latter. Russians rarely visited Egypt, and the High Aswan Dam they later helped to build was not there to prevent the Nile from rising and falling bountifully each season, overflowing the land in great waves of life-giving silt. Above all, the air was brightness itself, falling from an azure sky, its color gem-hard as all colors in Egypt are: the emerald fields, garnet and topaz desert, the sea shifting between sapphire, turquoise, and tourmaline.

True, I perceive the changes from afar, in the tales of travelers, in news reports. But mutability endures as the law of laws even if time slows and speeds to the mind's metronome. Did Egypt then alter its ways as much in my father's or grandfather's time? I think not, and take Abu Simbel as witness or symbol. Only fish swim now where temple and statue stood, flooded by Lake Nasser, for three millennia, intact. Still, sawed free from their original rock, these monuments of slow time rise again, different, reassembled on higher ground. Will their stone memories survive the wrench, recall the place they once held beneath the man-made lake? And for how many more centuries, now that the air of Egypt has lost its wondrous dryness, will these statues continue to greet the rising sun?

Luxuriantly cosmopolitan—almost as much as in Durrell's *Alexandria Quartet*—pre-Nasser Egypt has now gone. Cairo itself has become a place of unspeakable pollution and occlusions, "crumbling under the weight of its people," the *New York Times* reports. Yet Egypt has also remained the same. After a revolution, a presidential assassination, four wars and a tripled population growth within half a century, what has really changed there beyond some streets and squares renamed? What profound political or cultural reforms? This, then, is the paradox of "developing countries": they seem hardly to develop at all. As for the already "developed" countries, they develop more and more. Thus the tensions between them threaten war, may trigger a holocaust.

Meanwhile, Eternal Egypt endures . . .

MUNICH

Every day, I write, or try to write, from eight to one; in the afternoon, I sometimes see the sights of this sprightly city, where work and pleasure inspire the human measure. More often, though, I read in a book. I have consciously brought few books with me here; for in writing this autobiography, I knew that I would require acolytes of another kind.

This tardy reckoning, though, may evade both the old Egypt I knew and the new Egypt I ignore. Still, my feelings run strong, flow in channels surprising in their twists: anger here where I expected none, reconciliation there where I thought least to find it, bemusement veining a mental landscape like the delta of the Nile. And I wonder how all these emotions touch my American career as "teacher," "critic," "humanist."

Perhaps I have brought few books with me here out
of sulk or spite, or an access of professional angst. But
I did bring some of my old notebooks through which I
browse. I come upon these notes, written some thirty
years ago:

I am first a man. Asked to define my philosophy or politics,
I always state my name.
But I am also a teacher, and my responsibility adheres to a
vision of the human adventure, not to a canon, method, or text.
Great teachers have something to teach. That is a given like
grace, or else earned by a great effort of the spirit.
No life wholly satisfied in literature càn bring to it the highest vision. No life wholly fulfilled in criticism can bring to
literature the deepest insight.

Brave words, rare thoughts, that even so heroic a man
of letters as Jean-Paul Sartre, in his autobiography *The
Words,* finds illusory.

Yet when I read my fellow critics, sequestered like
myself in academies, I want to recover part of my young
ambition, callowness and all. Some professors devote
themselves to ethereal Ironies; others, in desperate re-
action, to prove the World exists, kick Language, thinking to stub their toes on a stone. Yeats rebuked the
scholars: "Bald heads forgetful of their sins." But humanists can be scholars and more than scholars, and
must recall what turbulence makes the spirit whole. Can
humanists learn to dream again, and dreaming wake to
mediate actively between Culture and Desire, Language
and Power, History and Hope?

Enough lamentation. As I write this book, I turn away
from the cant of criticism and its bad prose. I read,

instead, a page or two of D. H. Lawrence's *The Sea and Sardinia,* or Freya Stark's *Perseus in the Wind,* or Isak Dinesen's *Out of Africa.*

Eternal Egypt: this is no mere alliterative phrase of school or travel book, but something closer to a curse, a fate. I remember a "feudal" land, which a nineteenth-century Russian novel would evoke more precisely than any medieval romance. I recall a landscape breathtaking in its spare beauty, a strip of green winding with the Nile through endless sand. I hear the peal of peasant children laughing, and see the somber faces of their elders, which could suddenly explode in merriment or fury.

I walk at dusk down a rutted road on our Delta estate. The road is narrow, its fine dust nearly caked; deep draining and irrigation ditches keep it on either side straight. A fellah in his early teens, feet dangling from a donkey, approaches on his way home. Seeing me, he dismounts with reticent respect, then notices the donkey's absurd erection, a blue-black thing curving nearly to the ground. He shouts, lashes the beast with his switch, then rides again into the gloaming, his voice now a derisive wail.

I stand back from the big convict in ankle chains. He swelters under a sun gone mad with its own heat, wielding a mallet I could never lift. The cords in his neck swell and his arms knot as he arches his body to bring the iron down on rock. He wears a skull cap woven of the same rough stripe covering his chest. His feet, like pulp, bleed among broken stones. Guards with red fezzes and loaded guns stand at attention as my father nears. The convict barely glances at him; his amber eyes rest on me instead, beyond seeing. My father says to the sergeant-at-arms: "Take that man to the prison hospital. Don't cane his soles till his feet heal."

I listen rapt to my French tutor who is telling me "The Adventures of Thumbalabava." Monsieur Monier gesticulates, making up the story as he goes along each week, and the story always reflects on the lesson of the day. But my tutor never speaks to Ahmed, the Nubian servant who lets him in. After the lesson, I go with Monsieur Monier to the Club, and watch him hurl the javelin, which hums and shivers in its perfect arc across the turf. Monsier Monier is the javelin champion of the province, but in our house Ahmed bangs the door, mildly, every time he shows him out. Indignant, I protest one day to Mother who says: "*Ma'lesh, Ahmed travaillait jadis pour la Compagnie du Canal de Suez.*"

Egypt was feudal; it was no less colonial. Many years after, I heard that Mamelukes used to skewer "insolent" fellahs on great iron spikes, that Egyptian policemen and prison guards caned the soles of criminals so that they could never walk again, that in the bougainvillad villas of La Compagnie Universelle du Canal Maritime de Suez, in Port Fuad, foreigners who plundered ancient Egyptian treasures flouted the laws of the land. To some, everything was permitted.

"But why?" I asked my father repeatedly.

"It's the way of power," he would quietly reply. Then one day he added: "But also remember Champollion and the Rosetta Stone. That's power of a different kind." And with one hand he made a fist, with the other an open palm as if proferring some invisible gift.

I think of the Rosetta Stone. Entombed now in the British Museum, it remains for me a master key, waiting to open the lock that keeps knowledge chained to power, language to tyranny.

———◆———

[Tyranny] is a familiar fact, explained to the child when he becomes a man, only by seeing that the oppressor of his youth is himself a child tyrannized over by those names and words and forms of whose influence he was merely the organ to the youth. The fact teaches him how Belus was worshipped and how the Pyramids were built, better than the discovery by Champollion of the names of all the workmen and the cost of every tile.

Ralph Waldo Emerson
"History"

———◆———

There is a violence learned early by every child. As I escaped Egypt on the *Abraham Lincoln,* creaking now in the long, gray swells of the Atlantic, I thought of my father, my mother, my uncles, and why I had so fiercely longed to leave them all behind.

I think I loved my father. He played with me throughout my childhood, his games a spontaneous art. Later, he taught me many things: how to fight with fists and knees and head, how to write with a split-reed pen dipped in ink, how to cut prickly pears and play chess so that I could hold him to a draw. When I fell recklessly from my tricycle, scraping elbows and legs, he would furiously shout: "*Ahsan, ahsan.* Next time you'll learn." But a glint in his eye belied his fury. He taught me also geography and history, how to swim and shoot an air gun, how to scorn mendacity, especially my own. Sometimes, when

I brought back from school a near-perfect grade of 18/20, he would feign astonishment and ask: "Oh, did you lose those two points on the way home? They may be lying in the street still."

But my father had another side, a black, glowering temper that could ruin his lessons, especially in math. He would suddenly rage at an error, slap my face, and snap his pencil on the page while correcting an equation. (Later, as an engineering student, I avenged myself by airily solving for him problems he could not begin to understand.) Did I, in my exorbitant pride, ever forgive my father for slapping me a few times in my boyhood? Can I, out of inverted pride, ever forgive myself for having done the same to my son? There are wounds that fester at the very root of our being, so deep they neither hurt nor heal.

My mother taught me French—English I taught myself, and liked it of all my "subjects" best. She taught me how to wash, eat, dress, and how to address all my elders with a courtesy she, like so many adults, could lack. She allowed me to pinch her, my early vice, though sometimes she lost patience and pinched me back hard. She was pretty, vain of her youth as a mother, tight this side of parsimony, less curious than my father and less eager to please. She prized ambition more than learning, honored tenacity in the world. What, then, did I receive from her? A certain grimness of purpose? Or did I come to value what she disprized: knowledge, generosity in all its forms? And why must we obscurely pit parent against parent, and so violate our trust, our life?

As for my uncles, they were an outrageous bunch, more truculent on my father's side; spendthrift and genial, rather unlike my mother, on hers. Yet they all buzzed continually with emotions, threatening suddenly to sting. Throughout my childhood, there were familial quarrels and squabbles about money, marriage, land, children, friends, politics, anything that could inspire argument or indignation, or, for want of better, mere reproach. I suspect that my family, as a whole, lacked a certain inwardness, a certain privacy of vision, which Egyptian culture tends to begrudge. The Civil Service jobs that some held brought them more boredom than power. Their lands, tilled by distant ghosts, yielded revenues which my maternal uncles prodigally spent on green-eyed courtesans in Budapest, or at the green gaming tables of Monte Carlo. Life, then, demanded some vehemence of feeling, continually renewed. This vehemence lurks in me still, dreadfully at the ready. I do what I can to shape it, control it, and doing so have acquired a habit of aloofness, countering this terrorism of the heart.

◆

MUNICH

The German papers proclaim it in headlines: the American hostages have been freed at last from Iran. Without vanity or braggadocio—could the French press have resisted either?—the papers also refer to the secret mediations of a German diplomat. Evidence of interdependence once again. But I feel both wrath and relief at the news, and try to envision, beyond this madness, what lies in store for our transhumanized earth. Planetized by ubiquitous technologies, the world retribalizes itself by fractious wills and desires. On one level, im-

manences; on many others, ruptures, indeterminacies
of every kind. Terrorism: the baleful break in our epoch,
the obscure schism in our private lives.

I brood over all those posters in the Munich *Bundespost*
stations, showing the smudgy, crumpled faces of young
German terrorists still at large. What fury, hope, or deprivation lies beneath those pallid skins? But faces beget
faces: I recall others, in Selma, Alabama, lined to jeer
the civil rights marchers of 1965, white faces twisted as
in a lewd dream.

Ah, something in me irrefragably knows that despite
all the differences of faces and places there is a will to
power or being, unceasing, a fanaticism of the heart, in
myself, my parents, my uncles, in all my unborn sisters
and brothers, from which history is made—and continually unmade.

———◆———

My childhood lay, I later realised, in an invisible field
of force: British colonialism. True, the phrase *El Ingileez*
would sometimes catch my ear, carrying some hint of
menace or obloquy. But as a child I had no aversion to
the English language itself, nor to its native speakers
who sometimes visited our house. Power, real power, I
then sensed, rested elsewhere: in my father's burly presence, in experiences which the body recalls before the
mind.

The power of my father was, in fact, provincial. As a
governor, his duties required him to walk on frayed
ceremonial carpets, inspect local police troops, bestow
dreary trophies at the annual *gymkhana*. Yet authority
somehow adhered to him as he strode about, carrying
a silver-headed cane that excited me more than all his

other badges of office. For the cane concealed a rapier, stealthy and sharp, unknown to all—so I thought—but Father and myself. This weapon has etched a particular scene in my memory.

We were strolling toward evening by a field of dense sugar canes. Father held my small hand in his left hand; his right, as usual, held the cane. Suddenly a mottled yellow viper slithered across our path, then inexplicably stopped, rearing its triangular head. It swayed ever so slightly, fixing two jet, unblinking eyes on me. I shrank behind one of Father's knees while he, hesitating for a moment, stood still. Then, softly, he slid the rapier free, and in one continuous movement impaled the viper through its head, stepping on the flailing tail to hold the beast at both ends to the ground. Writhing insanely for an instant, the thing terrified me as if it were still free. When the sword came finally out, red drops glistening on its steel, I felt a strange thrill. It was like a clear note trilling throughout my own blood, fear that had suddenly turned into glee.

This glee had another side, some childish compassion that did not yet recognize itself. I had seen playmates dismember live birds and insects, rapt as in a secret ritual, and experienced first fascination followed by active disgust. We came sometimes to blows; sometimes I fled. "You're born under the sign of Libra," an English friend of the family, whom I called Aunt Cecily, once told me, holding my open palm in her hand. "You will always defend justice. But remember, scales go up and down, and justice is like a swing."

Another scene comes to mind; it evokes less pity or justice than force, force coming suddenly, hideously to light. Here is its background. As a small boy, I sometimes accompanied my father on his visits to outlying districts, leaving my mother back in the gubernatorial residence. In these remote regions, we stayed at *Esterahat el rye,* austere rest houses designed originally for irrigation inspectors who administered "the waters of life." Such houses seem all to have been built from the same functional plan. Outside: olive, plastered walls with bright green shutters; inside: hissing carbide lamps that gave off a bluish light, mosquito nets large as white elephants, massive Victorian furniture that melted into restless shadows in the night. And invariably, behind high, spike-topped walls, the houses stood in the midst of immaculate gardens, as if to prove that the miracle of the Nile could bloom anywhere.

In the morning, my father would leave for work; the single resident servant would go shortly after to market. I would be left alone to play in the garden, imagining myself sole master of some ever-changing landscape— of turrets or jungles or ensorcelled isles—obeying my airy will. Out in the open, in a sunlight softened by the early hour, the aura of earlier visitors to the *Estraha,* which lingered inside, vanished. Only inhuman presences moved about: lizards, hoopoos, sometimes a stray tomcat or lost baby porcupine, and rarely, a scorpion, against which I had been strictly warned, and which I loathed as I loathe all insects.

On that particular day, the garden all a-dapple, I saw two big scorpions meet in the gravel path. Squatting at a distance, stick in hand, I watched their combat transfixed. They locked into an amber mass of claws, mandibles, and curveting sting, now still and lucent in the sunlight, now flailing in convulsive fury. They struggled there to some strange, immemorial end; and when one finally staggered away, leaving the other palpitating on its back, I could not bring myself to kill either with my stick. I did not eat that day, feigning a sickness that was, like life itself, really unfeigned.

Many years later, I recalled the incident and thought: "You're a Libra born close to the cusp of Scorpio. There's also in you a touch of sting."

The sting of colonialism is rarely visible; its ravages lie within. The British rumored themselves "civilized colonials," and so they were, compared to the Spanish, French, or Portuguese. Subtle, distant, and discreet, the British divided to conquer, and acted ruthlessly in whatever touched their needs. How else could they have ruled Egypt for seventy-five years?

Like every schoolboy, I grew up with fierce fantasies of liberating Egypt, which remained for Nasser's Free Officers Movement to accomplish in 1954. But, like most schoolboys too, I had never directly experienced the "oppression" of the British. Once, before my birth, they detained my father three days for some unacknowledged deed; that single feat provided my family with its myth of heroic resistance for years. Once, too, during the war, when Rommel stood near El Alamein, I saw a red-nosed "Tommy," taunted beyond endurance by two Egyptian students, knock one of them down. That, and a few tanks rumbling on the way somewhere, was all I saw of British power in Egypt. Even their large barracks at Kasr El Nil, displaced now by the Nile Hilton, might have blended easily into Cairo's cluttered landscape except for the high-flying Union Jack. Urchins on the street would sometimes look up and, seeing a British soldier lean casually across his window bar, make some wildly funny face or obscene gesture which the man above invariably ignored.

The British, I repeat, divided to conquer; in this, the squabbling political parties of Egypt seemed eager to oblige. Ultimately, Britain ruled through a decadent royal house and a landed oligarchy, inept, venal, and vain. After the revolution of 1952, after the confiscation of royal properties in 1953, schools and hospitals rose rapidly everywhere, more in that year, Sadat claimed, than in the preceding twenty. Still, I wonder: had Britain brought illiteracy and disease to Egypt in the first place? Did it impose poverty on the fellah for millennia? Who makes imperialism possible? And how healthy, free, or affluent are Egyptians thirty years after their liberation?

ON THE COLONIAL COMPLEX

Like some invisible worm, the colonial experience feeds on all those seeking redress for old wrongs and lacks. Self-hatred, self-doubt, twist in their bowels, and envy curls there with false pride. "*Baladi, baladi,*" Egyptians cried to dismiss someone uncouth or vulgar, forgetting that the word means "native." But Egyptians also feigned scorn for Europeans whom they strove to emulate. Was European skin a little fairer? "Allah, what difference can it possibly make? My cousin is fair." Was European literacy, or power, or technology, preeminent? "*Ma'lesh,* never mind. Those *frangi* perform no ablutions and eat pork. How foul!" Thus the tacit principle of the Colonial Complex: to extol only such differences as serve oneself, other differences to depreciate or ignore. Thus, too, the

Colonial Complex both constitutes and institutes its necessary bad faith: necessary for resistance, self-respect, sheer survival, yet shady, shifty, nonetheless.

This sentiment can sweep entire nations—witness the resurgence of Islam from Morocco to the Philippines. Atavistic and often brutal, the surge still offers the Faithful a new dignity. It does so by voiding five centuries of their colonial histories, by rescinding, together with modernization, all that humanity has striven in that time to attain. Neo-Islam speaks thus to the West: "Neither your imperialist past nor your technological future is relevant to us any more, and your present dominance is already on the wane." This challenge, perhaps less challenge than solace, can not escape a certain historical paranoia.

As for myself, out of pride or pain, pain at seeing the legacy of colonialism maim so many, I resolved early never to give it a place in myself.

◆

MUNICH

Why have I really come to Germany, to Munich of all places, to write my "autobiography"? Germany has never held colonies in Arab lands. Is that a reason? Sally and I have had our qualms about Munich, and have slowly, gingerly, entered Germany after the Thousand Year Reich. In this we are not unique; even Germans have learned to fear Germans. Lost in a jungle of bicycles in Shanghai, Günter Grass, in *Headbirths*, suddenly asks: "What if, from this day on, the world had to face up to the existence of nine hundred fifty million Germans, whereas the Chinese nation numbered barely eighty million. . . . Is such a thought possible? Is such a world conceivable?" But how German is it, finally, this violence of human order, Walter Abish asks with the precision of art?

I return to Germany to worry this dismal query, and construe the deep grammar of my heart. But perhaps I return also, in this reflexive year especially, to recover my own youth in Egypt. For like many Egyptian students, more frantic than informed in their idealism, I saw Rommel in 1942 as a liberator. Surely, we thought, the enemy of our enemy must be a friend. Yet when the Allies defeated the Desert Fox at El Alamein, the same students, changing allegiance, found in Americans, if not liberators, new models for their aspiration. We consumed Coca-Cola, devoured the *Reader's Digest,* affected RayBan aviator glasses, and gawked at all those gangling, loping, gum-chewing, foot-propping GIs who began to appear in Cairo, their drawl so different from any sound we had ever heard. Now, after forty years, that same drawl, heard accidentally on a Munich street, evokes all I am willing to call "home."

◆

Home, they say, is where the heart is. But three hearts beat in me. One existential, a little Faustian; one utopian though politic; one Orphic, almost mystic. Those three hearts, I suspect, beat in us all, pumping blood into the near, the middle, and the far distance, farther than any receding star. And when one of these hearts falters or fails, we shrivel a little in our humanity.

My trouble has always been the middle distance—knick knacks; bricolages; family relations; social interactions—where mind remains captive to nature as well as to history. To compensate for my gnostic warp, I recall Flaubert's little fable of the vultures and the obelisk:

Often you see a tall, straight obelisk, with a long white stain down its entire length, like a drapery—wider at the top and tapering towards the base. That is from the vultures, who have been coming there to shit for centuries. It is a very handsome effect and has a curious symbolism. It is as though nature said to the monuments of Egypt: "You will have none of me? You will not nourish the seed of the lichen? *Eh bien, merde!*"

Still, it remains "a very handsome effect," which Flaubert renders more handsome still through language, imagination, the mind's countless insubstantial eyes.

2

Solitudes: 1925–1941

THOUGH BORN IN CAIRO, I spent my childhood in country houses that float in my memory like dream clouds, now dim, now darkly aglow.

A civil servant, my father acted first as legal counsel, then lieutenant governor, then governor of various Egyptian provinces. As he gained in seniority, his provinces became more prestigious, larger, or closer to Cairo. But "prestige" demanded that we move every three or four years. Such transfers became moveable crises; for my mother insisted on redecorating each gubernatorial residence, whose previous tenants she always found a little *baladi*, a little countrified. In these strange mansions, the father was absent for the day, the mother alone with her boy-child. A prescription for happiness? Ah, but my mother was absent in her fashion too.

As a "modern woman," she dressed smartly, attended functions, received visitors who spoke French and brought news from Cairo, sometimes from Geneva or Paris. A small brunette—the family called her "our Sylvia Sidney"—she was neither melancholy nor bored, only *nerveuse*, vaguely dissatisfied. Seldom sentimental, she was also incapable of dreaminess. But she could liven an afternoon with sly wit, or darken it with subtle reproach. In the end, she remained self-absorbed.

I still recall her pet, a small, moist-nosed, yapping spitz, which she called Bijou—or Lulu. Neat, fluffy, and immaculately white, it struck me always as a conceited little beast. But Mother fussed over it continually, whereas I wanted to smash its black button nose with my toy shovel, teddy bear, or rubber-tipped arrow. In retrospect, I think my mother may have found in Bijou—or Lulu—some reminder of her pampered life as the youngest child, only daughter, in a large household.

How rough-hewn my father seemed by comparison! But his large features (perhaps a touch coarse, my mother would sometimes imply), his sulfuric temper, driving energy, and aura of authority—all these concealed a distinct weakness, which my mother knew and I came to hate: a need to ingratiate himself, a kind of shy obsequiousness. Whence this strange vice? Thence my own willed truculence? And how did my mother, so much less curious and questing, become the steelier partner over the years?

Happy families may be all alike, as Tolstoy says, and every unhappy family unhappy in its own way. But no child really knows where his or her parents live their deepest lives, lives concealed to the child like the dark side of the moon.

Munich

I detest showing my unfinished writings; I spare even Sally, which amounts to sparing myself. Some rare evenings in Munich, though, after a good day at the desk, after an *intimes Abendessen,* warmed by Sally's gaiety and her culinary arts and a glass or two of Schladerer schnapps, I hand her a scribbled page tormented by many erasures.

This evening, her eyes fall on the lines about my mother's spitz. She laughs: "Will sibling rivalry never end?" Then in a darker voice: "How was your mother *really?*"

I do not answer, knowing that the reality of my parents, long dead—dead to me perhaps before they entered their grave—must evade me just as I have tried to escape Egypt. And I wonder to myself: "Did Oedipus really slay the Sphinx, or did she perish of boredom, repeating the same riddle to all those human hordes whose bones lie bleached in the immanent desert?"

Outside, the Munich night is soft, green-black.

———◆———

A dry sun reigns over Egyptian landscapes, as Amon Ra reigned over the gods of the Old Kingdom, his right eye the clear day, his left eye darkest night. But my earliest memories of the countryside revert to a moist darkness, a darkness alive with birds and beasts.

I slide back to a fringe of time in Faiyum. Rigid with terror, I lie in my crib under a ghostly mosquito net, while owls hoot to one another in the night, one perched on my window ledge. The terror rises slowly in me, like a liquid filling the silence, crests just before each ululation begins, then ebbs quickly to rise again.

From Beni Suef, I carry images more mysterious than frightful. Strange birds, called *el waak*, settled in a great eucalyptus tree before our house. Their long wings fluttered among the leaves at dusk as they filled the tree with their cries. Invisible, they left behind only greyish droppings to betray their passage. Once, my father shot a bird down, and it came wheeling to the ground, its round eyes regarding me like an ostrich in mortal surprise.

I descend to another moment, in the deserted cellar of our *ezbah,* our Delta estate. The black, acrid air is suddenly full of wings which snuff out my candle. I remember my grandmother saying: "Stay away from that cellar, it's full of *wotwat* (bats), and nothing but *tabl el baladi* (tin drums) will get them out of your hair and face." In panic, I lunge and dodge toward the white crack of light under the cellar door, and keep running till I fall down sobbing on the sunny lawn.

Later, a boy still, I became an ardent hunter, and would look in vain for some quarry worthy of that taut, tingling passion, strangely akin to prayer, which hunting awakens. But big birds were rare in Egypt. Storks and pelicans circled too high, out of shotgun reach; eagles, the few remaining outside hieroglyphic cartouches, had long vanished into their mountain fastness. Kites remained, with their rolling, metallic cry; crows, more cunning than any fowler; hoopoos, flicking their crests like coquettes with a fan; and *abu erdan* (white egrets) glistening in the rice fields. Yet none of these satisfied my hunter's longing, which reached farther than my BB gun and, later, my single-barrel fowling piece. Longing for some wild, inhuman life, wholly beyond my ken.

Animals stalk our past, our prehistory; but in populous Egypt, worn smooth by time, wild animals belong only to myth. The lion, the leopard, and the hippopotamus, the ostrich, crocodile, and giraffe, are seen on temple walls—or else in the Cairo zoo. True, in my childhood, gazelles still bounded gracefully on slender desert legs in Upper Egypt, and jackals came down to the villages at night, like harbingers of the underworld, sniffing carrion. But wolves had become nearly extinct, except one I shall never forget. Caught in the glare of our headlights on a desert road, it turned on the pursuing tire and snapped, snapped gloriously before vanishing among basalt rocks. As for crocodiles, only once, I recall, did a monster slip through the old Aswan Dam, provoking a state of emergency in the province. My father quickly sent out sharpshooters in a motorboat, ready with rifles and net. The beast was captured, bound and crated, sent off to the Cairo zoo.

Father was himself a skilled shot, easily dropping birds on the wing with his twelve-guage Purdy, which I liked to unpack from its felt-lined leather case and assemble before his critical eye. Sometimes, he let me accompany him on a duck shoot. He would tip-toe to my bedroom before dawn and find me already awake, lacing my little hunting boots up to the knees. We would rush through a breakfast of thick, hot porridge, fried eggs over baked Egyptian beans, and black tea, and ride out in the grey light, the earth reddening at the rim, to meet the hunting party at lake's edge. I would keep close to my father, who would whisper to me explanations as we went. When he missed a teal or mallard in flight, I looked down in shame and fury; I glowered at the bullrushes. Father would sense my feelings, which unsteadied his hand, and ask me to trail another gun for a while. At sundown, colors of gold and lead melting on the horizon, the flat-bottomed boats, gravid with their booty, slid silently toward the reedy shore; and I would feel weary, weary, wrung out by my emotions more than by hunger, heat, or fatigue.

I learned much from these hunting trips. I saw loyalty, endurance, skill, saw much pettiness and greed as well. I witnessed cruelty, the cruelty of men even to their retrievers. I came to love the acrid smell of gunpowder in empty shells, which I fitted on my fingers, blackening my nails. And I came to dislike captive animals, and to despise any beast domestic to man. In our park, a menagerie contained, at various times, monkeys, gazelles, foxes, hedgehogs, rabbits, hamsters, snakes, peacocks, pelicans, pigeons, ducks, and silkworms. But I lost interest in each soon after its imprisonment in shed or cage.

Haunted as a child by sounds in the dark, I became a daylight hunter, stalking my own emotions even as I pursued animals, so alien yet so inward with our being. After a hunt, or even a day at the zoo, I dreamt exorbitantly, doing my nocturnal work to account for some violence at the heart of creation. But there came in my late boyhood a day, unannounced, when I resolved to be neither hunter nor hunted.

On Evolution

Will all the animals of Egypt, of the earth, vanish as human beings continue to multiply, as nature turns into history and history into symbols, languages, traces of (im)pure mind? In Egypt, Teilhard's vision of "hominization"—the earth turning into a human noetic space—finds an egregious case.

Consider: Some fifteen millennia ago, the Agricultural Revolution occurred in fertile crescents, perhaps on the banks of the Nile. The river rose and fell each season; the fellah used his neolithic *fass* (hoe) and *shadoof* (water bucket), as he does to this day. The Egyptian calendar gave time a human measure about 4241 B.C. and King Menes founded the First Dynasty around 3400 B.C. Egypt left aeons of nameless nature and entered wordy history; and everything there, once done, was done again. Everything, that is, except unpredictable change. Thus, despite the fanatic conservatism of the earth, something always happens, something new and strange. This we call evolution.

The landscape, first dumb, becomes mythicized, then historicized, then conceptualized, even as the fellah maintains his Stone Age ways. Nothing escapes human intervention, the mind's touch, not even microbes. (The High Aswan Dam, Egypt's largest intervention in its nature, has aggravated the *bilharzia*, or schistosomiasis, now eating the fellah's guts away.) Thus technology, increasing the dominion of mind, can also lead its makers astray. And instead of the few million Egyptians who throve on the Nile for millennia, forty million now jostle to eke a living from a dream that the High Dam has in part betrayed.

Forty million inhabitants, procreating every day. Everyone knows that a room holding one person is not the same room with four or forty-four. Intense human interactions—so many brains, biographies, desires in a narrow place!—augment differences in the body politic as well as syncretism in culture. "In principle, much of this is not new," Daniel Bell notes. "What is distinctive is the change of scale. . . . All that we once played out on the scale of the Greek polis is now played out in the dimensions of the entire world." This is Teilhard's "planetization," a process more problematic than he presaged. For even as the world interpenetrates, aspiring to become whole (the One), it breaks into shards (the Many). Can the earth sustain this deadly dissonance and still compose a gnostic music of "pure mind"? Will soul ever sing to soul, im-mediately, like holy ghosts in pentecostal flames?

———◆———

From hunting I moved on to bigger game, self-entrapments of solitude. Since I was tutored at home for the first ten years of my life, I rarely had playmates, except when we visited Cairo or Alexandria; then I sought out my cousins in endless play.

But I forget Saidiah of Sohag. She was seven, my first bitter love. Mother would later deny this vehemently: "*Non, c'etait* Mimosa, *ton premier amour.* You played together naked on the beach at Juan-les-Pins. *Tout, tout bronzés.*" Mimosa? She remains for me the memory of a memory, perhaps even Mother's invention, to prove her priority. I dare not wonder what woman Mimosa became lest I lose myself in blind labyrinths of time. But I do recall Saidiah, full of scorn. Violet eyes, pale yellow hair, she was no doubt the gift of some wandering Crusader to Egypt. My torment was her delight. Twisting her little finger solemnly into mine, in ceremonial recognition of our *khusmah* (estrangement), she would turn her back and ignore me for days. Finally, pride conquered by despair, I would complain to her father who served under mine as lieutenant governor. He would chide her gently; she would pout; we would become reconciled. Then, to avenge herself, Saidiah would treat me still worse. Incensed, I would now myself seek a break, twisting our little fingers again while she gave me an evil smile, knowing that I would run to her father, we would be reconciled, and that she could then treat me more derisively than ever before.

Spurned by Saidiah, I sometimes turned glumly to play with the servants' children. The game I chose was called *El Taab*: four slabs from a palmtree branch, green on the outside, on the inside white. Each player throws the slabs in the air, and anxiously watches them land. Four green, you are King; four white, the Grand Vizier; three of the same color, you "pass in safety"; but woe if you land "two and two." Then you become Prisoner; the King would decree your punishment, the Grand Vizier execute it. Needless to say, after a quarrel with Saidiah, I velt vengeance rush to my small breast. As King or Vizier, I clamored for harsh sentences, thinking: "Let the Prisoner's blood be on her blonde head!" But then, I would see my playmates screw up their faces, they who hardly dared to punish me when *I* lost. A rush of shame would displace all else, then ebb, leaving me limp, crumpled, like a soiled rag.

◆

MUNICH

As I write, I read again my old notebooks—rare, spare jottings of thoughts and experiences but never of memories—which I have kept since my emigration. Thus two streams of time flow through my mind: one of recollections that find their source in an Egyptian childhood, the other an abstract, laconic gloss on my life in America. The two streams now surge through our months in Munich, months of work, music, sensuous pleasures, of *lived* time moving in still another stream. All three, in confluence, enter this book, a fourth stream still, or perhaps a shoaly river, itself made of many currents.

I reread what I have just written about Saidiah (which happens also to be the name of the secondary school I attended). I smile, thinking of the sexual truculence of our age. Truculence? In the end, it comes to this: either we like our lives or else nothing avails, nothing sustains.

During a particular period in my childhood, my parents knew the Fury of Matrimony. But that moment passed, and their mutual devotion lasted more than half a century. Still, in that period, my mother would have preferred her only child to have been born a girl. Once or twice she admitted to me as much, more wistfulness than spite in her eyes. She gave me doll houses—my father forbade the dolls themselves—which I found breathtaking in their precise detail, a magic realm inhabited secretly by kindred spirits. (Later, though, I developed intense distaste for puppets and fetishes, for objects of every kind.) She also dressed me often in frills of velvet and silk, and at the slightest excuse would clothe me in fancy costumes. I would strut about, to conceal how intensely foolish I felt, pretending to be a Spanish toreador, Renaissance courtier, or Arab chieftain.

One of these costumes became a trivial cause célèbre in our house. The occasion was a formal visit of King Fuad—stern and puritanical as his son, Farouk, was dissolute—to Sohag. It was decided that I should present the king with a great bouquet of dazzling white roses. But how should I dress to make my offer? For days, my father and mother argued the question into the night, their voices pursing me to bed, through the soft edge of sleep. I can not recall, have no doubt repressed, the fantastic sartorial visions they brought to their debates. I remember only their weary compromise: a turn-of-the-century police cadet suit, black gabardine with red silk piping, golden buttons with the Royal Arms of Egypt, starred epaulettes, dress sword, gaiters, and stretch pants tied beneath high-arching black boots.

King Fuad came up the Nile in his brilliant white yacht *El Mahroussa* (the Protected One). The ship glowed at night like a floating galaxy, outshining the spangled, colored bulbs and floodlights on each shore. The next morning, brass bands struck up as the yacht began to dock. Mounted police, their lances trimmed with green and white streamers, lined the embankment while their officers pranced their horses back and forth, swords at rest, glinting in the sun. Headed by my father, the reception party stood nervously waiting on a pier swathed with vast oriental carpets while the ship churned the muddy water, nosing into place. Finally, the portly king, clad in a tight pearl-grey *redingote,* stepped down the gangplank on small, elegant feet. I felt a quiet push at my back, and walked up to him, beribboned bouquet in hand and rubber in my knees. Somehow, I managed to bow from my small height—I had rehearsed this with my mother endlessly—bow without sweeping the ground with white roses. In a whisper, I welcomed the king to Sohag. With the flicker of a smile, he received the bouquet, said *"Mutashakereen"* (we thank you), and passed on. Suddenly, after weeks of excitement, of timorous expectation, I found myself standing on the pier, free and unburdened, alone.

Does freedom compel us always into solitude? I think of Prince Fayez, one of the royal family's numerous black sheep: even as an adult, he kept running away from home. Young, fair-skinned, shy, with Circassian eyes and a handsome aquiline nose, he exuded adventure, a certain gentle recklessness. Periodically, he would disappear into the Sahara, trying to cross it on foot alone. Then the *hagganah*—the crack and incorruptible Nubian desert patrol, with slits on their temples "to improve" their piercing vision—would set out on white dromedaries to find him. And they would bring him back, barely alive, his lips swollen and black, his face burned raw, skin cracked, self-poisoned by drinking his own urine. He would spend a week convalescing in the state hospital of Sohag, and another in our house, before returning reluctantly to Cairo where his royal family waited coldly to receive him.

Prince Fayez felt at home in our house. He hated fuss: "Please don't touble yourself, please . . . ," he would whisper. He seemed entirely surprised that anyone should think his "explorations" odd. Once, I summoned my courage to ask him in French: "But Prince Fayez, why do you really keep going into the desert alone?" He looked at me, wide-eyed, a soft shadow across his face: "One must do something, after all." Then the shadow passed and his face became serene like a saint's.

Fifteen years his junior, I too thought sometimes of running away from home, but reached no farther than the garden gate.

INTERLUDE

Moses, Mohammed, Saint John the Baptist, the desert with all its prophets, anchorites, and holy men. Given harsh grace, they glimpsed in God's bare and inexorable mirror the lineaments of soul. A part of me has always longed for their parched state, and for the fierce solitude of the nomad, moving across timeless sand. That sand is glass, and also, Paul Zweig says, pure "space, the horizontal abyss." But like Zweig at the end of his *Three Journeys,* I have always returned. The desert waits.

To whom, to what, did Prince Fayez return? The hush of scandal, regal decline.

After King Fuad, King Farouk: what mutation of the genes or psychic spasm creates such gross contrasts? As a youth—svelte, languid, pretty like a school girl with soft oval face—Farouk captured every heart. Till he swelled into a tub of lard.

The story of the royal family encapsulates that of Egypt itself: prodigal, corrupt, cruel sometimes, flashing in rare moments of splendor. (In my day, nothing flashed brighter than the "King's Crimson," a vibrant orange-red paint that marked the royal fleet of Rolls-Royces and Cadillacs, before which Cairo traffic opened like the Red Sea.) Ineffectual *khedivs* favored a slack, landed aristocracy, and their joint profligacy bled Egypt till colonizers, in a feeding frenzy, closed in like sharks. Yet the royal family itself traced its origin to a colonizer of a different stripe. Mohamed Ali, a ruthless Albanian adventurer, became pasha of Egypt in 1805 after wresting it from the High Port; later, he wrested also Syria, Cyprus, and the Sudan from the Ottomans.

According to legend, on the first of March, 1811, Mohamed Ali Pasha dined on a sumptuous carpet stretched over the groaning, bleeding bodies of six hundred Mameluke officers whom he had invited to a banquet in his Citadel—and slaughtered. Thus he consolidated his rule. The legend has the ring of history—or rather its endless moan. Origins, Freud and Frazer tell us, are steeped in gore. Even the foundations of the old Aswan Dam, like those of the Pyramids, cried for human sacrifice to cement their stones in place. Hence *ginns, afrits,* and *marids* still haunt these sites at night, calling for blood, the only answer to blood.

Someday, history may cease its wail, and the earth, forgiving as always, may soak up the blood of kings and all the blood they have shed. Someday, somehow . . . Meanwhile the fellah sings mournfully in the fields:

> Hast thou resolved upon strangling me,
> O Allah?
> Loosen the noose!

◆

MUNICH

I woke up the morning after writing the foregoing pages with the vague memory of a dream. God and his Viceroy had come to fetch my soul to its final place. God

was large, infinitely large and sad, and his Viceroy had
the mien of a statesman—was it Reagan, Schmidt, Sadat?
No one spoke as we ran indefatigably, airily, through
mountains and valleys, through rivers, caves, and chasms.
I can not recall where the journey ended—some misty,
craggy place by a white sea? But I recall precisely the
feeling that clung to me for nearly an hour after I woke
and walked about, not wishing to write or speak: a feeling of immense compassion, without trace of self-pity,
which included everything, everything, even God and
his Viceroy.

After Sohag, we moved again. My father served briefly
as governor of Port Said, then administered, succes-
sively, the Delta provinces of Dagahliya and Qalyubiya.
These were more populous, more gracious than the
provinces of Upper Egypt, but softer, vaguer in their
beauty.

At Port Said, I returned to the sea. I had first seen
the Mediterranean during my summers in Alexandria.
There I sometimes stayed with Uncle Fuad and Aunt
Hania, sharing with my cousin Nihad a bedroom in the
attic children's quarters. Dormer windows, bleached
parquet floor, often grainy with sand our sandals brought
home from the beach, vague scent of ribbons and lace
from the room of Nihad's elder sisters, Hoda and Esmet.
Barely awake, the sound of slapping, swishing waves
flowing still in my dreams, I would rush to the window,
fill my lungs with the warming salt air, and strain to see
the flagpole on the beach. A green pennant, joy of joys,
meant a safe sea; red meant some danger, restricting
children to wade; black banished everyone that day from

the water. Red and black, rare enough in Egyptian clime, broke our boyish hearts.

But it was really in Port Said that I learned to swim, ride the surf, dive below high rollers before they crest, and tumble unhurt in the sand-choked, churning wash of breakers. I learned there to love the sea, love it as much as the desert that claimed part of me. For sea and desert met and spoke each to each on the coasts of Egypt, spoke through aeons before man could speak.

I came also to distinguish liners passing through the Suez Canal: the big, black and tan Pacific and Orient ships bound for India or Australia, the elegant white cruisers of the Lloyd Tristino, the tricolor *paquebots* of the Messagerie Maritime. I sailed with them all in my daydreams toward exotic climes, far meridians.

Above all, I became aware of the marks of European colonialism imprinted everywhere on Port Said: on the gleaming white marble headquarters of the Compagnie Universelle du Canal de Suez (really, a universal, a cosmic corporation?) with its great blue and gold dome, and its signal flags flying from high, brass-trimmed masts; on the bustling harbor of tugs, tenders, liners, cargoes, ferries, and menacing, lead-colored battleships, aloof from the rest; on the old luxurious Palace Hotel, burnt in the Anglo-French invasion of 1956, with its immense seafront veranda, covered by a wooden porch four stories high (in the hotel dining room, I first learned to bone a *sole meunière*); on the carriage of top officials in the Compagnie, coldly, impeccably correct.

These officials, though, felt obliged to attend the annual Water Games in which their company competed, and over which my father presided—as he did in Upper Egypt over the *gymkhana* of racing horses, camels, donkeys, mules. The games took place in the harbor, where festive floats de-

marcated a water "field," encircled by launches, punts, row-
boats, all chock-full of spectators. Rivalry with the
Compagnie was particularly tense in water polo and water
jousting. (In the latter, "knights" clad in bathing suits, carrying emblazoned wooden bucklers and supple, rubber-
tipped bamboo spears, jousted from high platforms erected
on boats rowed by eight brawny men.) Each time the national team, in green-and-white skullcaps, scored a goal in
water polo, each time a "knight" of the Compagnie fell
from his "steed," arms and legs flailing, a cheer ripped the
air before subsiding into the usual patter of applause. Officials of the Compagnie applauded too, barely touching
their palms.

But childhood rarely dwells in rivalries, colonial dis-
putes. I retain from Port Said other images of sensuous
recall: sliding down a sea chute to find myself astride
the glistening black back of a dolphin; waves lapping
calm hulls while urchins shout to passengers on deck
and dive for bright coins below; British naval officers
marching in crowded streets, as crisp as their white,
starched uniforms; the smell of ship linoleum, sound of
husky harbor horns, feel of giant twine cables, creaking,
straining between ship and shore in a rising breeze. Did
I already have a premonition then that I would someday
sail from here, on a war-battered Liberty Ship, bound
for my version of the American Dream?

◆

INTERLUDE

I find these entries on America in my old notebook:

Europe possesses a past; America makes one; but the past
America makes becomes elsewhere in the world an optative

future. That is, America, alembic of time, distills the future in the present, and so permits other nations to choose their destiny. This does not always win gratitude.

The historic role of America? Beyond language, nation, and clan, to create (precariously, violently) a new order of diversity. Neither "melting pot" nor "rubbish heap," neither sociolect nor idiolect, but the One and the Many mediated dangerously, toward a uni-verse. The world's dream?

If America seems relatively apolitical, is it not because traditional politics (power and interest institutionalized in older forms) has become historically obsolete? More precisely: in what sense is an advanced technological country "postpolitical" rather than "apolitical"?

———◆———

I became more aware of Egyptian politics in El Mansura, capital of Daqahliya, then rife with student protest. Students believed themselves to represent the only political awareness in Egypt. Their volatile demonstrations, in which I later participated, could express sheer deviltry and fun, a carnivalesque relief from crushing studies. But their riots could also bring a government down.

At that time, the perennial grievance was British colonialism, a grievance that the patriotic Wafd Party, headed by Mustafa el-Nahas Pasha, sought always to inflame. Eloquent, wily, and bold, el-Nahas also considered himself a "man of the people"; whenever he visited a village or town, the entire population would pour out to cheer him—except landlords. Such visits became the stuff of a governor's nightmares, sometimes the stuff of his unmaking. Pressured by the prime minister in Cairo, who would be pressured by the king in turn, governors sought to "contain" the junkets of el-Nahas without actually constricting his movements, since he might someday sweep into power and avenge himself. It was a game of perilous balance, won only by consummate pols.

El-Nahas visited El Mansura early one spring. For a whole week before his arrival, the town alternately sulked and seethed. Schools shut down; *sooks* (markets) swelled. Helmeted police, on horse or foot, patrolled the streets, wielding long supple canes or leather-strapped cudgels, carrying iron shields. But the students had cunning and surprise on their side. Once, driven home in an open *décapotable,* my father suddenly found himself surrounded by a mob of faces, black as gunpowder, ready to flare. He stood up in the car and spoke to them for an hour before they dispersed. Once, too, the son of the lieutenant governor, a boy my age, was jostled by a gang of students who lay in wait outside the primary school gates. The gang had intended to ambush me; when they discovered their mistake, they gave the boy soft licorice candy and sent him home.

In the end, the bloody confrontation that my father had tried to avoid came. El-Nahas surged into El Mansura on the crest of a roaring sea of *gallabiahs;* crowds rampaged through squares, through streets, smashing windows, hurling bricks and ordure at the police. Anger and fear mingled, and mingling turned into rage. Canes and cudgels sliced the air, people fell, trampled by hooves or boots. Police lines buckled, then broke like mud dikes before a flood. Rifles suddenly appeared, fired over the rippling crowds, then at their feet. By day's end, six people lay dead in the streets, four students in their teens. No one counted the wounded.

Was it, after all, a clash of useless passions? I confess it: on that fateful day in El Mansura, I felt my loyalties torn between my father and his foes. Three years later,

Mustafa el-Nahas Pasha became prime minister of Egypt. My father was forced to resign. Thereafter, we lived in Cairo, in "reduced circumstances," as my mother liked to say.

MUNICH

I write about this crucial event in my parents' lives some forty-five years later. To refresh my sense of names and places, I consult Frauen Dr. Emma Bruner-Traut and Vera Hell's *Ägypten: Kunst-und-Reiseführer mit Landeskunde,* which a blonde, bosomy saleswoman at Hugendubel's—she has recently visited Egypt herself—assures me is *der beste.* Seven hundred and eighty-four thin pages, countless maps, sketches, illustrations. The authors, Egyptologists both, know my native land as I never have nor will. Yet I continue to construct this "autobiography," block by fictive block, like a pyramid raised by treacherous slaves. Can my shaky edifice commemorate those Egyptian students dead in the street? Do my words re-colonize the fellah, who will never read them, as do all these learned books I read?

After my father's forced resignation, we lived in Cairo. Our seven-room apartment occupied the top floor of a two-story, fin-de-siècle brick and grey stucco building facing the river on Shari el Nil, near El Gala bridge. No high-rises obstructed then the sun, the eye. On any day, I could see from our balcony the old Semiramis Hotel across the Nile, and beyond it central Cairo, rising eastward toward El Mokattam Hills, toward the Citadel, and the mosque of Mohamed Ali with its twin, slender (too slender) minarets and great central dome. A large vegetable garden abutted on the southern side of our house, owned by a Coptic neighbor, shy and prodigiously rich. To the north, across a side street, lay a flowery, open-air café, where the Cairo Sheraton now stands. (In that café, Om Kulsoum, *el bulbul* [nightingale] of Egypt, sometimes sang, her wailing voice pure and high pitched). Behind the house, to the west, I practiced bicycle fights on my Raleigh in an improbably empty lot. In that house, I lived ten driven, yearning years, attending first the Saidiah Secondary School, then the Faculty of Engineering at the University of Cairo.

That decade proved turbulent for my parents as well. Never quite wealthy, they seemed comfortable enough even in their "reduced circumstances," and later became affluent again as my father devoted himself to my mother's estate, gradually buying out her brothers till *el ezbah* belonged to us. But in the initial stress of adapting to their new conditions, they quarreled with one another, quarreled with my uncles, who quarreled back with gusto. Suddenly alone, my parents began to discover how they could live together without provincial pomp or rural retinue. The difference in their ages may have been more than twenty years. (I cannot be certain: my mother fiercely kept her age secret, and would later pretend that she could pass as my elder sister). That difference in age exacerbated their incongruous sensibilities.

My mother "did errands." The chauffeur drove her downtown every weekday at ten. She would return by *ghadah* (lunch), which Egyptians take at 2 P.M. when government offices close for the day, and say: "Ouf, I have done nothing, nothing at all." My father brooded.

Sometimes he called on influential politicians who vaguely promised to restore his position. Erratically, he visited Abdeen Palace to inscribe his name in the Royal Book on national holidays. More often, he read fitfully in his library, stacked with big bound volumes of Macauley and Thiers; or solved intricate problems on a portable chess set that folded into a lacquered box, its tiny, ivory pieces fitting snugly into holes.

As for myself, dreamy, a little *sauvage*, tutored at home and mildly pampered for the first ten years, I experienced much grief when I began to attend government schools. These proved intellectually demanding, socially bruising, physically dismal, proved altogether traumatic for me. At the grilled, lead-hued gate of the school, which shut at five minutes past eight with frightening finality and opened mercifully again at five minutes to four, the parental Rolls or Daimler might wait for the most privileged pupils. But once inside, these abandoned all hope. Jostling with the rest, they relied on their wits, fists, and unbreakable skulls—a quick, sharp blow with the head to the enemy's nosebridge—to absolve themselves daily of cowardice, effeminacy, or simply good breeding. In the brief recreation periods, the younger boys played *el beel* (marbles), viciously throwing their nickle leaders at a triangle full of bright, multicolored spheres. Older boys played *fudbal* (soccer) with a makeshift lump of old socks, delighting to kick each other in the shins. Lunch was a predatory affair, wolves and hyenas, the stronger or hungrier fighting for inedible gobs of glutinous matter while *el alpha* (the monitor), disdained by all, tried to establish some order of precedence around the table. (For many, poorer pupils, this was their only meal for the day.) Extracurricular activities? Suspect. Character development? Absurd. The fit survived, and everyone studied grimly or else fell by the way.

Not quite ten, I entered the lowest grade of Saidiah. The youngest boy in class, I wore short pants; a new, red *tarboush* (fez) barely concealed hair parted on one side. I sat at a rickety, sepia-colored, wooden desk, ink-splotched and carved-up by the *canifs* (pen knives) of all my predecessors. When the teacher stepped briskly into class, we all clattered to our feet and saluted, hands to fezzes, standing till he ordered us seated. The lesson began, and as in schoolrooms around the world, excitement and misery mingled in the period, which sped or dragged till a hand-rung bell struck the hour.

Directly behind me sat Tawfik, the class bully. He was fair, almost creamy of complexion, not particularly muscular. But he could glare ferociously or snarl, displaying a snaggle tooth, and he fought with reckless glee. At once, he began to smile at me, making a slow, pumping motion with his hand, his thumb and index forming a circle. I smiled affably back. Afterwards, I discovered the meaning of his lewd, homosexual gesture. We fought, of course, and I lost—gashed lip, blood filling my mouth, ribs aching for a week—though not so badly as to brand myself a pansy nor so well as to discourage future strife.

That first year in school became my initiation to social reality. It certainly wrenched, remade, my character. I woke every morning with fear in my guts, in my feet; I ended each day with an infinitesimally stronger sense of my endurance. I could not share my pain with my parents; I could not stay away from school. The year passed, the next came, the misery remained. Then one day I made a stunning discovery: I had lost my fear. I discovered also that by striking out first I could win most fights. Sensing, really believing, that I had nothing to lose, I found that I had accidentally won everything, almost everything. Suddenly, I began to excel in my school work, standing near the top of my class. Suddenly, too, I became popular: boys asked me to join their secret bands and warring gangs, practicing roughhouse pranks. I declined, my old bitterness stronger than their new-fangled flattery.

Tawfik and all those boys who had bullied me for an eternity began to fade from my awareness. They also faded into a lower "form." (At Saidiah, the higher achievers were segregated into the same classroom or form within each grade. Thus pupils bound for the university moved from first form, first grade, to first form, second grade, until their last year in secondary school, first form, fifth grade.) But a few others—Talat, Ibrahim, Roshdy—remained within the tight, invincible circle of friendship through my school and university years, until exile, marriage, age, dispersed our ways.

Though I belonged to no racial or religious minority in Egypt, I was tormented more than if I had been a freak. What have the tormentors of my boyhood become? No doubt, some have grown into upstanding men, model fathers to their sons. Were they to recall the pain they once inflicted on a boy, they might now wince and squirm. Or was that pain but some exchange for a lack they themselves as boys endured? Lack or warp, something there tempts us to indulge a nameless evil; we torture purely, like art, for its own mysterious sake.

On Self-Heedlessness

Evil and fear have no dominion over the self-heedless. So sing the perennial philosophers, casting their words to the four winds.

I translate this: accept death, self-dissolution. The desire for immortality, the undying self, hell itself contracted in the eternal "I am"—these drive demons, from Lucifer to his lowest acolyte, vampire, werewolf, and ghoul. Thus most superstitions testify to *self-persistence*, the weird power of the past in ancestors or revenants. And that "power of blackness" in old American literature, does it not betray the self-encapsulation of spiritually gifted characters, arrant in their desires, from Wieland to Ahab?

Still, out of such arrant desire life wills itself into being. And so we are. And being, we live in fear, though a deep breath could clear that fear away. For fear comes with need, that human integument binding us badly each to each. Hence the paradox of freedom: he that loseth his life shall find it, as the Gospels and the *Bhagavat Gita* say. Ideal for transcendent warriors and saints.

Summers brought relief from the rigors of the Saidiah Secondary School. My parents sometimes traveled to Europe; sometimes they vacationed in Alexandria or Port Fuad. But much as I loved the sea, I loved best to spend my summers alone with my grandmother on our Delta estate.

Long, idle days, full of sunny projects; soft summer nights, echoing with stories and laughter; nature gracious, appeased, without sting, without those locusts descending like a black cloud from heaven in Upper Egypt. This was a time out of time, will-less and free, irrecoverable except as a charmed space, the green garden each child carries within him, perhaps to inhabit again only at the instant of death.

Our *genenah* (orchard) was the most treasured part of the estate. Rows of orange alternated with peach trees in a rectangle larger than several football fields. Two latticed vine arbors intersected over the orchard, meeting at the center in a high, octagonal kiosk, painted blue and orange, which served as a perch for sparrows, swifts, hummingbirds, doves, and hoopoos. All these fed rapaciously on ripe grapes and peaches, and like local orchard thieves had to be driven away by guards banging cymbals in the harvest season. But at other times, the orchard breathed peace, the fragrance of incipient fruit. In its dense geometry of shades, I learned to play hide and seek alone, to double myself between row upon straight row of trees, and to recognize the fluttering shape of each, startling myself as I came upon my Other around a bend.

Other times, I preferred to follow storks circling high in the immaculate blue sky, a swirling, dotted cloud which would finally glide gracefully away into some far-off space, beyond my reach or ken, leaving me with a bittersweet pang for the rest of that day. Or I would fish in one of the *ezbah* streams with a hook made of twisted pins, catching the whiskered *armut* (catfish), which I threw back in the muddy water in revulsion from its thick, slithery body and flat, primeval head. Or I would follow the line of deft cotton pickers in the field, singing as they plucked the long-threaded "white gold" of Egypt from its dried buds, and intervene when supervisors tried to whip, with a thin stalk, girls who left unpicked cotton in their wake. Or I would join the cooks in the kitchen to make delicious mango or watermelon ice cream, turning by hand the syrup in a metal beater covered with cracked, salted ice, till the liquid became mysteriously gelid. Or I would sketch the twenty-room country house in which all my maternal uncles had been born, using charcoal stubs on large, rough-grained paper sheets, seeking to capture some quality of it as it rose, solemn and solitary, above the shimmering green haze of the fields, the mud village of "our" fellaheen— I never set foot in it—slung low behind the house, except for the conical turrets of pigeon houses. Or I would play ping-pong with Samia, a pretty, henna-fingered, bare-footed, laughing servant girl of twelve, whose long earrings tinkled as she moved, and whom my grandmother forbade to accompany me anywhere out of her vigilant sight. Nothing else those summers was forbidden to me, except swimming in the *bilharzia*-ridden streams.

After luncheon, I liked to steal away upstairs and read. Since my grandmother refused to climb the steep stone steps of the house, the whole second floor remained mine. I read while others napped. In some unfurnished rooms, books piled there on books and across buckling shelves; magazines rose in teetering columns from the floor; and the scent of thick, musty paper greeted my nose in closed, high-ceiling rooms, evocative in its way as the smell of smoking cartridges under a dawn sky. Here was the scent of words, verbal dreams. Pell-mell, I found French novels, classical Arabic poetry, English detective stories, German technical manuals, medical books in sundry languages. I found old wrinkled maps of the earth, glimmering celestial charts, inscrutable surveying deeds, spectral anatomy drawings, still-lifes in ornate, gilded frames, and sepia photographs of mustachioed men and crinolined women, some with *yashmak* (veils), whose names I never came to know. Rows upon yellow rows of the *National Geographic* magazine took me around the world in an hour; and huge folios of the *London Illustrated Gazette* unfolded before me the Great War, Ypres, Chalon, Amiens, Verdun, the Marne, mud and blood filling trenches of battles that rumbled still in my family's talk.

I read riotously and consumed myself as I read. I obeyed no principle but irresistible whim, took no witness other than the lazy, afternoon flies. And I came down for supper only after my grandmother, calling from the stairwell repeatedly, threatened to close the kitchen for the night. At table, I ate silently, my head wounded, swaddled in a huge bandage of make-believe. But my grandmother would joke and scold, piling food on my plate, and menace me with the evening's game of *tric-trac*, till I returned to her side.

Strange country pleasures these, that enchanted a boy even as they sapped his will. For I endured no greater wrench, until much later, than returning to school after an indolent season at the *ezbah*. Season of green dreams.

INTERLUDE

In my old notebooks, I find many entries on Imagination, Fantasy, Make-Believe. I ponder these entries with the skepticism of age, scrawling laconic counterstatements in parentheses:

The Imagination is the teleological organ of evolution. It predicts change, it directs change, it fulfills change. (Modern literature also reveals the Imagination to be a corruption of life, a disease.)

Lying sunders the Word from the Flesh. By a sound, a phrase, we manage to annul reality. This is also Imagination. (Precisely. It is also language in its intrinsic "counter-factuality.")

The women in my life—mother, grandmother, some others—have always wanted me to stop reading. Is woman hostile to Imagination? (Not Sally.)

Some summers, my parents took me to Europe. Though I think of myself as a "westering spirit," I retain only a few slivers of recollection from those prewar holidays:

—a stormy passage to Marseille, interrupted mercifully at Mother's insistence in Lebanon, from which we returned (how did we return? I recall only my stomach everted, and nausea, nausea and rain unending) . . .

—on another voyage to Europe, a quaint hotel room in Vienna where I "experimented" by setting newspapers on fire in the bathtub whenever I found myself alone, and mixed my parent's medicaments in glasses or aspirin tubes, silent, intent, like an alchemist . . .

—huge, flapping Kurhaus awnings in Carlsbad, painted porcelain mugs from which everyone drank the abominable water, and my father's smile as he simpered at pretty waitresses, till my mother glared at him . . .

—on still another trip, my acrophobia discovered with shame, surprise, in the steel *ascenceur* of the Eiffel Tower (when my palms turned clammy, I put them in my pocket and tried to gaze insouciantly at the horizon, the crazy rooftops of Paris, the gingerbread Sacré-Coeur) . . .

—my father's explanation of the Underground system in London, and challenge to me to return to the hotel alone from Kew Gardens, which required changes at Victoria and Picadilly . . .

That Europe of my boyhood passes before my eyes like a film, now vivid, now suddenly blank. But the feeling I retain of it is of something infinitely strange though wholly familiar, something that inhabited the European languages I knew from childhood and the books I had read, something that called, beckoned.

A similar intuition colored my perceptions of Alexandria. Founded by a god-man, that city had been imaginary from the start, housing the greatest library, the highest *phare* (beacon), of the ancient world. Races and tongues mingled there more freely than in Cairo, that mingling inescapably erotic, like the perfume of bathing oils blending in a warm breeze with the sea's. The women—French, Italian, Greek, Lebanese—walked barearmed in the sun, their motions liquid like houris, yet stranger, more sensuous even to a pubescent boy.

But I did not think of women then; I built sand castles and cavorted with my cousin in the waves. Though younger by two years, Nihad was always *el alwal* (first in his class), and was constantly held up by my parents as paragon before my eyes. Still, we loved one another in common innocence, in the shared altruism of play. We remained inseparable, commingled in a sweetness of disposition, an ideal courtesy some children intuitively know. His adolescent sisters, Hoda and Esmat, left us to our boyish devices. Hand in hand, in modest display, they walked up and down the beach, gravid with their nubile mysteries.

Certain beaches in Alexandria had implicit status, which changed fashionably every few seasons. At first, Stanley Bey held the edge, then Glimonopoulo, then Sidi Bishr I, II, and III. (Now the beaches reach farther east, beyond El Montaza.) Status depended on many factors: the size of cabins and distance between each, the quality of sand, the clientele of the beach, and of course its distance from the town's center—the farther the better, since this clearly assumed a private car. Stanley Bey, a deep crescent lined with cabins in three tiers, attracted handsome young surfers, many of European descent; old Egyptian families considered it a little "fast." In contrast, Sidi Bishr II seemed staid; but its pale sand felt warm and silky between bare toes, and its commodious cabins permitted the family to lunch, nap, or play cards all day at the beach.

I liked Sidi Bishr II best because its mild, constant breeze rarely required the beach guards to hoist their dreaded black pennant. I liked it, too, because adults in our families—who avoided the sun, preferring to keep their skin light—stayed in their cabins, far from the sea's edge, leaving children to their games. Yet that intolerable moment always came, that dull, soft hole in time called *la sieste*. "It's too soon after lunch. Don't go into the water," our parents would sternly say. Then coaxingly: "Put your head down, *un petit quart d'heure*." But Nihad and I would squirm and twitch, till someone cried in exasperation: "If you can't sleep, be still so others can rest. Or go play. *But not in the sea*." Nihad and I would then steal away behind the cabins and whisper stories in the cool, silent shade. Or we would play "Tomix" (Tom

Mix) and "Kemenyar" (Ken Maynard) with cocked thumbs or Colts carved from driftwood, making up plots of Westerns no one ever screened. Or else we would seek out the cunning pistachio vendor to play "Even and Odd" with him and win as many nuts as we could from his bright glass and brass box. Until the time came again to rush headlong, sand flying from our heels, hurdling thin garlands of green and purple kelp, and dive into the glowing afternoon sea.

In the evening, all "the children" would dress and go with a governess to the Hotel Casino San Stephano where the morning rituals would be reenacted with subtler variations. Older boys and girls strolled in the Casino gardens in clusters, casting around knowing looks, all innuendo and shadow play. The younger children, like myself, scraped their knees at *patinage*. Later, under a quickly darkening sky, all would troop in to watch the latest Hollywood movie in the open-air cinema. There on a wall transmuted into screen would be the fabulous faces of Greta Garbo or Carole Lombard, Clark Gable or Robert Taylor, Loretta Young or Hedy Lamar, Tyrone Power or Errol Flynn, faces of stars flickering under the stars.

And the next morning would bring another cycle in the round of summer play, till the close of the season, the *rentrée*. Yet with that headlong hope boys carry in their breast, I came to feel, despite those wrenching departures from seaside or country estate, that summer's end was but the start of all my days.

———◆———

Increasingly, I discovered in Saidiah an outlet for my energies. I endured its dreary, disinfected classrooms and execrable lunches because the world opened itself to me again as it had on those long, silent afternoons when I read at *el ezbah*. At Saidiah, though, the auto-didact in me encountered odd and exacting masters.

Most pupils perceived only the ludicrous quirks of their teachers. One, dubbed "The Klaxon," kept tapping his hip pocket during class to check on his wallet; another, called "The Clutch," reached for his crotch and glared to stress a point in the lesson; a third, nicknamed "The Bullet," fired chalk pieces with the accuracy of a high-powered rifle at nodding or chattering boys. Other teachers, however, evoke images of richer hue.

I recall Mr. Miller who taught us the King's English, and conveyed a certain hurt radiance even to the rowdiest spirit. His pale, pinched face and distant, sunken eyes rendered all the horrors of W. W. Jacobs' "The Monkey's Paw," and his flashes of mock braggadocio infused in *King Solomon's Mines, The White Company, Montezuma's Daughter, The Coral Island, Kidnapped,* and *The Prisoner of Zenda* a delightful irony without impairing their romance. He had a taste for things Gothic, a gentle way of shaming obscenity into silence. He may have also inspired me to the first prize I ever won at school: a handsome combination desk calendar and writing pad, inscribed, "For Excellence in English."

I did well in all subjects—except Arabic. Once, my total points in the marking period earned me second place even though I had failed Arabic. The headmaster came as usual to congratulate the three top pupils in class. He called on the first, and walked up to his desk to shake his hand; he called on the third, and did the same. Then he called on me. Pausing as if in great perplexity, he lowered his brown, watery eyes and softly asked: "Why, my son? Are you *rumi* (Greek or Roman, any foreigner really)?" I did not fail Arabic again, though I never did more than pass it; and when I missed Highest Honors on graduation from secondary school, I blamed it bitterly on my battered native tongue.

Highest Honors were attained by placing among the top ten students in Egypt in the nation-wide baccalaureate examinations. The "top ten" were separated from one another by a few points, sometimes only by half a point; and often, when two or three pupils tied for the same place, the ranking would skip, say, from first to fourth, keeping "the ten" only ten. I placed thirteenth, which guaranteed me entrance to any university, but not the inscription of my name in golden letters on a plaque, hanging in the main hall of the Saidiah Secondary School. (To this day, I regret the omission with a small, occasional twinge that takes my self-irony by surprise.)

The baccalaureate examinations resulted annually in a national trauma. Harsh, exigent, and inflexible, more French than English in their centralized character, these exams, lasting two weeks, remain the most strenuous I have ever endured. Administered across the nation in vast, silent tents, with endless rows of numbered desks and sawdust on the ground, the ordeal—indeed its very place—exuded dread. Watchful monitors prowled the aisles of that city of the living dead, construing any communication, any whisper, as an attempt to cheat. This brought instant retribution: a red mark in the corner of the examination book, assuring failure. Punctually at the end of each exam, the head monitor screamed maniacally his command: "Pens at rest! Pens at rest!" Any delay in obeying this doomsday cry brought again the red stigma of failure. Thus we raced against time as well as each other, raced ultimately against our own selves.

Failure meant a year lost and, far worse, shame. Students who failed sometimes committed suicide; others, in fearful anticipation of the event, would flee their homes, or simply collapse. Thus the great battles of Egypt were fought not on the playing fields of its public schools but under its examination tents. Were these battles really won? I have known piercing intellects among my classmates who have either emigrated or remained to find their minds brutalized by bureaucracy. I have known others who lost hope and quietly lapsed into cynicism, sloth, sensualism. Is the school itself to blame for this? Is Egyptian society? In some rude, outlying districts of Upper Egypt, an intelligent school child may aspire to a world centuries, literally centuries, ahead of the world its family inhabits.

Ahead?

On Knowledge

Knowledge is virtue, Socrates said; knowledge is power, Bacon rejoined. Renaissance humanists attributed to education everything from civic virtue to sexual courtesy, from aesthetic awareness to moral insight and even eternal life. In the New World, the educational premise sustained the American Dream for two centuries, though neither dream nor premise now escapes challenge. And in "developing" countries? The mandate remains practical, technological, illiberal—or else fundamentalist, sweeping away knowledge in the name of Allah, a *jihad* against history.

Between pseudo-technocracy and Islamic reversion, what, then, can avail? Something, I think, beyond nationalism, socialism, revivalism, beyond convulsive hope and each day's dram of despair. Yes, a sense of worth, relief from need, the will to change, and, withal, reverence for life, all life, whose staggering design we have barely begun to glimpse. Also: imagination, cognitive wonder, a faith in human gnosis. For though we learn and learn all our lives only to die at the end, that labor of self-perfection passes, as if by Lamarckian inheritance, into all the generations waiting to be born. And who knows but that such ceaseless labor, unremitting gnosis, accrues to the perfection of the universe? Thus mind transforms itself even as it alters the cosmos, and this, too, is "education": *the education of creation.* In this, scientists, poets, and mystics may be of one imagination compact.

———◆———

Cairo displaced the scenes of my childhood. I gave myself to the work of self-creation, self-recreation. Tensed in will, I learned to put away childish pleasures, put away even those privileged moments of being every child holds against time. Yet such moments inevitably return:

—*les jolies choses,* mysterious, iridescent objects made of ivory, glass, and gold, locked away in Mother's slender Empire desk, which she spread on a black velvet cloth before my rapt eyes, as reward for good behavior . . .

—the shrill *zagrat* (ululation) of peasant women, rejoicing in a wedding or birth, filling the air with a sudden, terrible thrill, an intensity of jubilation so sharp that I felt tears rush to my eyes and urine tingle for release . . .

—a moment of murderous complicity with Father, as we sat alone at the desert's edge, and saw from afar two brigands steer their camels our way, then veer off again when Father lifted his Purdy and held it visibly across his lap . . .

—sudden fear, its taste warm, acrid, in my mouth, when I saw the creeping shadow of a tree late one night, my head pounding with rumors of an escaped maniac in the region, then sensing all fear ebb before my faith as I recited the shortest *sura* in the Koran . . .

—the reckless, exultant feeling of a summer day, when I threw myself fully-dressed in a *bilharzia*-infested stream to defy perversely my fate . . .

This last exultation casts darker shades. Was it a premonition of some evil, some enforced self-alienation in myself, solitude aspiring secretly to death? Many years later, I read with a chill of recognition how Adrian Leverkuhn, in Mann's *Doctor Faustus*, set out to acquire from his hetaera, his Esmeralda, the syphillis that, Nietzsche-like, rotted his brain. Thus he excluded himself from the sacrament of life. In spiritual pride and radical impatience, we may wait too soon at death's door.

3

Resolutions: 1941–1946

CAREERS. WE DRIFT into one, elect another, obey yet a different call, then wake one day to find ourselves cast on a distant shore. We work all our days to make ourselves, or remake the world, and with luck may stumble on a brilliant hour, unmaking all our pain. Mercifully, we see nothing ahead.

I received my baccalaureate in the spring of 1941. I wanted desperately to enter El Harbiah (the Royal Army Officers School), modeled on Sandhurst, and drive the British out of Egypt. Had I had my way, I might have joined Nasser's Free Officer Movement, or perhaps lain in a desert grave, among the red hills of Sinai, after the first Israeli War. But my parents would not hear of it.

"El Harbiah," my father scowled. "With your grades? You can enter any faculty, medicine or engineering. Why waste your brains?"

My mother was more indignant. She hated every hint of war as much as any whisper of *déclassement*.

"Who goes into El Harbiah now? The lower orders. And some rich delinquents who can't manage anything else."

To me, El Harbiah stood for discipline, idealism, a sharp, clean edge to cut off the rot of Egypt. Radical surgery, not technocratic reform: that's what this gangrenous land needs, I thought. I was at the age of sinister purity. But my parents would have none of it. Obscurely, they sensed I struck at their mode of being, sought to undo their lives.

That summer, I sulked and skulked. My parents left for Alexandria; I stayed behind in Cairo, alone. Sometimes, I would ride a tram to the end of its line and idle about, there where the rails ended, bending back upon themselves. Sometimes, I would go out into the desert, away from the feculent city, away from the small emblems of domesticity, the soft impedients of relatives. And I would burn a dry palm leaf, past the tracks of caravans, in memory of unknown desert warriors, anchorites, ravenous saints.

When autumn came, I joined the Faculty of Engineering of the University of Cairo. Though its course would last fully five years, the degree, I consoled myself, would lead me out of Egypt. Out of Egypt!

MUNICH

Meditating on warrior-saints in Germany, I think of the degenerate metaphysics of the S.S., the gloom of a thousand, private *Götterdämmerung*, the dubious seductions of Wagner's *Parsifal*. Unregenerately romantic in some reach of myself, I still seek home-made clarity, lucidity of every sense. In that mood, I pick up *The Ronin* by William Dale Jennings. Like a samurai's sword, this story slashes through political cant, theological dross, polished bright by the tact of Zen. For this, I had brought it to Munich.

The story concerns a giant, ruthless ronin who becomes, despite himself, a saint. Miscreant, this "league-leaping mutant" of the spirit finally seeks forgiveness, not through immolation but service, through life itself. "A strange election's taken place and I've been chosen to act out some Mystery without a single When or Where or Why!" For ten years, he digs a tunnel for the peasants of his region through a stone mountain, digs alone, only to find that his tunnel breaks out in the sheer face of an abyss. "Most would-be saints have a prior destiny with Waste." Yet the Groundhog of Paradise, which fears its own shadow, looks upon him. Sensing that he possesses "the holy habit," the ronin avoids that "show of selflessness sure to bore everyone for all time to come." At the end, he simply vanishes into the night, knowing in his marrow that even "the gods have no use except to serve."

With something like envy, more dangerous than envy, I wonder if I could ever sustain such ascesis. Earlier, the ronin had abandoned his last need, the woman he once loved. "I did it! I did it!" he shouts at the night skies, running barefoot through broken fields. Could I ever do the same?

The question sends through me a shiver, as if death had touched my skin. For I know him now as death, or one of his emissaries, who calls us to an impossible rigor, a purity cross-grained. Yet sitting here—yes, even in Munich, where another name for purity put Europe to

flame—I cannot shut out completely the spirit's exorbitant claim.

———————◆———————

Soon after my admission to the Faculty of Engineering, I took up religion and sports. I took up both
fanatically.

In my youth, in my day, it was considered crude, even
boorish, to display religious zeal. No one, of course,
spoke against Islam, nor would a nominal Moslem deny
its central creed: "There is no God but Allah, and Mohamed is the prophet of Allah." But the history of Egypt
proved conducive to tolerance, even if each sect believed
itself alone elect.

My family considered itself Moslem as naturally as it
accepted a rainless day. Yet its various members drank
alcohol, gambled occasionally, fasted irregularly, never
visited Mecca, and seldom prayed, not to mention those
other peccadilloes which human beings share in a so-
dality wider than any faith. For my family, for an entire
Egyptian milieu, Islam simply defined a cultural inheritance, backward sometimes, sometimes uncouth, yet always a source of pride, pride that concealed its prejudice.

This prejudice took root in social rather than spiritual
grounds, ultimately sinking into that clotted underground which nourishes all human fears. In Bulgaria,
polyglot and polytheist like Egypt, Elias Canetti experienced during his childhood many prejudices, including the prejudice of Sephardim Jews against other Jews.
In Cairo, I saw upper-class Moslems discriminate against
other Moslems more subtly, tenaciously, than against Copt
or Jew. Fairness of skin, in shades perceptible only to an
Egyptian snob, connoted descent from Mameluke,

Turkish, or Albanian ancestors, some of whom had held feudal estates since the times of Saladdin. As for religious observance, not to mention zealotry, that could be left to servants and fellahin.

None of us ever knows enough to cry: "I reacted against this . . . I became that. . . ." I know only that for a year I became unbearably devout, flouting my piety, relishing my parents' discomfort. For what parent can bring himself to say: "Son, you are too virtuous for your own good or ours"? Had I been by nature an adherent, I might have joined the Moslem Brotherhood then, which Nasser later outlawed as terrorist. Instead, I fasted, kneeled toward Mecca, and gave charity to beggars with an inner arrogance that should have delighted Iblis (alias the Devil).

But was it all just adolescent revolt, waywardness, spleen, at best young pride testing its fettle? The quest for verity, probity, justice, for an ethos to counter centuries of deprivation and defeat, the spirit's thickest sleep, was then, as it remains now, a crux of politics as of moral life in Egypt. Nor was my "Moslem Interlude," as my mother came to call it, all protest or all ascesis. I roamed Cairo in search of its legendary mosques where I could pray: Amr ibn-al-As, named after the first Arab conqueror of Egypt; El Azhar, tenth-century seat of Islamic learning; Ibn Tulun, which reputedly stands where Abraham sacrificed the ram for Isaac; Sultan Barkuk and Sultan Hassan, the last perhaps the masterpiece of Islamic architecture in Egypt; and Mohamed Ali Pasha, highest on the Cairo hills.

Roaming those ancient quarters of Cairo, I discovered much which had been denied me. I saw the quotidian city, crowded, sordid, insistent, color-crazed, throbbing with a sensuous energy that left my senses dazed. I became a tourist, wide-eyed and fastidious, in my own native place. I walked through the bazaars, brimming with strident vendors and garish wares, fearful of some contamination I could not quite name. I evaded the bold, *kohled* eyes of street women, the fluttering touch of peddling children, the mournful frolics of cripples. I saw, as in the *Arabian Nights, el sakkah* come around the corner, bent double beneath his great water-buffalo skin, selling water for a few piasters. And I saw the merchant of *kharoub* stride among the crowds, gaily bedecked in red and white, silver castanets in one hand and bulging beaker strapped across his chest; in the beaker's mouth, a big splinter of ice cooled the crimson juice. Once, even, I saw the crowd open in a hush before the local *fetuah* (strong man). He stomped the ground and glared, veins bulging in his bull's neck. A ferruled staff—thick as his penis, someone whispered—preceded him menacingly, and a purple scar cut across his cheek and brow. An unceremonial dagger showed in his wide, braided belt.

In the *fetuah*'s quarter, his rude word made law; in the mosques, another spirit, immanent, serene, reigned. The mosques I visited appeared nearly empty, so vast their masonry and quiet their space, creating a larger inner space. Straw mats spread from wall to wall, yellow and cool beneath my shoeless feet, like desert sand at sunrise. Here I could leave behind the confusions of the bazaar. Here I could escape my own nascent prurience: urgencies of sex, anxieties of venereal disease, phantasms of menstrual blood and female circumcision. Here I would experience an intimacy of being as I performed my ablutions, feeling the soft rustle of water flowing over hands, arms, feet, over face and scalp; as I heard the high wail of the muezzin drift from the minaret: *"Allah akbar, Alla-ah akbar, Alla-a-ah akbar,"* as I kneeled, facing the sacred niche southeast, then pressed my forehead ritually to the ground, astonished by its mute immensity. Yet even then—or do I think this only now?—a vein of hedonism laced my faith. This showed in Ramadan, season of extremes. Tempers could flash, especially in summer heat, and angry words would pass among friends. But those words soon would fade, forgiven, forgotten: *"Yallah,* it was only the hunger of Ramadan." From dawn to dusk, fasting kept the spirit edgy, lean; then, precisely at sundown, the Cairo cannon boomed, its echo rolling among the Mokattem hills, releasing all the faithful from their ordeal. Many of the poor were long inured to hunger, though in that holy month, charity sometimes supplied their needs. Many of the rich pretended to fast during Ramadan, yet gorged themselves at sunset, as if breaking their fast, before laying their jowls to rest.

Near sundown, I sat on the balcony reading the Koran, feigning indifference to the cannon's prandial boom, while Ali, in spotless white gallabiah and broad red sash, set the dining room table for *el fetar:* literally, break-fast. (Setting it thus beforehand, my parents agreed, Ali could later eat his own meal in peace.) I read the Koran, but my mind wandered away from its visions of the hereafter, rendered in resonant verse, to things mundane. I imagined the sideboard, inside, covered with walnuts, hazelnuts, almonds, and pistachios, all heaped in a bowl; figs, mangoes, grapes, and diverse, multicolored dates; or perhaps some cakes, *kahk* and *ghorayebah;* or perhaps sweets, *kunafa, esh-el-sarayah, amar-el-din,* jewelled with nuts and sugared fruits. Then I would wrench myself from esurient reveries, realizing that I profaned Ramadan, making it a gluttonous feast. Many hours later, at *el sahar* (pre-dawn snack), I would sleepily contemplate the spare tray by my bedside—bread, water, fruit—and would feel chastened again, austere. By the time Ramadan ended in the feast of *'Eed el Kebir,* with its orgies of sheep's entrails, kidneys, brains, hearts, roasted testicles, I loathed all that crapulence, in the name of Allah, which I had shared and seen.

Thus began—beginnings are lost to us always in mystery—a life-long rhythm of resolution and relapse, abstinence and satiety, puritanism with a wide sybaritic streak. Hurdy-gurdy of aspiration and need.

INTERLUDE

The puritan, it seems, solicits forever the hedonist, the Stoic invites the Epicure—in mutual disdain. Freya Stark says in *Perseus in the Wind:*

One wonders when the puritan first began. The cleavage of poly- and mono-theist, of hedonist and ascetic, of Epicurean and Stoic, of Catholic and Protestant, seems to be one of the genuine divisions of human kind. What first made the creature dissatisfied with that which for all the rest of creation appears to be sufficient? Perhaps it was the desert where "the barren earth entwines few tentacles about the heart. . . ."

Whatever the ultimate origins, the book of Genesis gives a summary of the repeated story: delight in external things, and then human hunger for truth beyond.

I think of myself as puritan, monotheist (if at all theist), somewhat stoical; but I honor luxury, Lucullan arts, women in their high finery, and concur with Brillat-Savarin when he claims, in *The Physiology of Taste*, that desire (*la génésique*) invades all our senses, our sciences, our arts. (In his introduction to that work, Roland Barthes goes still farther: need is animal, he says, but "*le luxe du désir*" entirely human, perhaps like language itself, the final attainment, or "perversion," of our race.)

I will not choose between the desert (protestant) and green, riparian vales (catholic). Ah, but I do love deep-sea fish and far-out swimmers, and creatures that drive themselves to the limits of their nature, there where nature waits to be remade.

◆

An adolescent finds rigor where he wills. I found it in religion, and found in sports a kindred tautness of spirit and gristle. I was not big for my age, but I was determined enough, determined to be determined, and agile.

I first learned to row a scull-and-four on the Nile, snatching the oar free on the beat, and twisting the blade flat from the wrist as the trolley-seat reached the end of the stroke. For months, our varnished skiff skimmed the choppy, mocha-brown river, passing full-rigged feluccas whose crews waved us over to "share their bread." (In Egypt, *uzmat el marakbyah*, the invitation of boatmen, has come to mean any ritual or impractical offer.) We darted beneath the rumbling steel bridges of Cairo which cast a moist, black shadow across our bow, and circled the islands of Roda or El Gezira. One day we returned to the bobbing clubhouse, moored across the street from my home, returned awash with sweat, back and thigh muscles aching and palms raw from rowing, to learn

from the trainer that we really lacked the "heft" to qual-
ify for the team's first scull-and-four. Sheepishly we dispersed, though we had so far clung together, avoiding
one another thereafter as if in mutual reproach.

I turned to other aquatic sports, where my light weight
mattered little, and made both the swimming and water
polo teams. In water polo, I offset my wobbly shots at
the goal by a knack for stealing the slippery ball from
opponents and passing it on to teammates with stronger
arms. Our entire team played with less power than speed
and cunning, and so won gold and silver medals inscribed with images of fearsome hippos, crocodiles, and
other Ancient Egyptian lacustrine gods. We wore the
medals ostentatiously around our necks, over our brief
black trunks, and dove and scrambled in the pool like
otters when the medals, torn off in play, sank gracefully
to the blue-painted bottom.

Incongruously, my recollections of water polo blend
into scenes of chess, and the smell of chlorinated water
can still summon memories of slashing opening gambits
and crunching end games. A coincidence lies behind
this transumption: the chess club shared its grounds and
coach with the swimming and water polo teams. Lolling
on the thick lawns of the pool between practice, young
mermen became masters of the chessboard, instructed
by swart, stocky, goggle-eyed Aziz Effendi. We called him
"The Cannon" because, purblind as he was without his
spectacles, he could slam irresistible, back-handed goals
halfway down the pool. But he could also pore over a
tangled chessboard and indicate quietly to the loser the
only dignified, perhaps even elegant, move. In the end,
Aziz Effendi may have been less privileged in his education than the young men he coached, yet he earned

their unswerving loyalty, unflinching respect. Was it because he offered us all an example of right action, high competence immaculate of self-concern?

It was in fencing, though, that I came thrillingly alive. Hardly a "sport," fencing compounded violence and ceremony, instinct and skill, engagement and distance. It demanded both grace and precision, yet its explosions of movement hinted at some desperate finality, as if all life hung on a *botte* or lunge. There lay its subliminal message: despite their masks, pads, blunted points, men acknowledged in that instant their capacity to deal or receive death. In that instant, they also found their bond. No accident, then, that Talat, Michel, Riyad, closest friends of my university years, composed with me the Faculty of Engineering fencing team.

We practiced in the Royal Fencing Club which occupied a white villa in the Ezbekiah Gardens, across from the old colonial Shepheard's Hotel. Talat's father served as chancellor in Abdeen Palace; Michel, from a wealthy Coptic family, drove his own Ford *décapotable;* Riyad seemed vaguely related to the royal family through his divorced mother, a cultured, decisive woman who powdered her face like a Kabuki heroine. All, in short, could afford the entrance fees to the club and, excepting Talat—his father had risen from a modest station, and enforced on his family old-fashioned manners—all spoke French more fluently than Arabic. But what we truly shared, even more than the shifting flow of friendships, was a "passion for the sword."

The Club's *Maître d'Armes* was a Frenchman called Prôst, and in his *salle d'armes* he reigned more absolutely than Louis XIV. (Or was he rather like some outrageous master of *kendo* who understood that certain tyrannies refine both spirit and sword?) For six months, he permitted us only to receive from him "*la leçon*"; he forbade us to fence or practice together. For a year thereafter we lived in dread lest, displeased with some awkwardness or error in us, he would order us curtly *à la douche*. He prohibited us from fencing with others till we lost all the "bad habits of our bodies." Later, even after we became collegiate champions, he ordered us out of the fencing hall whenever he sensed the slightest lapse in our skill or will. *À la douche!* Dismal interdiction, sound of scorn! Humiliated, with silent sympathy only from the old locker room attendant who warmed our clammy canvas suits in winter—like us, he was much ordered about—humiliated and barely sweating, we would shower and return sullenly each to his home.

I have often wondered why I should have cared so much to fence or not to fence in that somber, oak-panelled hall, its walls lined with bent foils, sabres, rapiers, its air smelling of sweat and fencing shoes and anti-skidding chalk. What atavism or romance conspired then to wound me to the quick? What idea of self-perfection took fire from steel rapping on steel, feet barely brushing the ground? For a few months before the Egyptian Intercollegiate Championships, I developed painful boils beneath my fencing arm. Secretly, I locked myself in our bathroom and slashed the excrescences with my father's open razor till they flowed in pus and blood. Then I bandaged my arm with thick cotton wads, kept fencing. One day, the boils vanished. The next week our team edged *El Harbiah* for first place. Gloating, I thought: "Well, dear cadets, if I can not join you, I will beat you."

Inebriate of success, I did not pause to think of Maître Prôst except in terms of vulgar gratitude. Who *was* this handsome Frenchman, after all, with blue-grey raptorial eyes and fluent muscles beneath alabaster skin? He had twice won the world championship in foil—so the rumor went. Now, in the prime of life, he lived alone in an alien culture, far from occupied France. Or had he come to Egypt expressly to avoid a war that humiliated his homeland? In his white flannel trousers and trim blue blazer, sporting the discreet insignia of the Royal Fencing Club in his lapel, he appeared always aloof, taciturn. Some said his stance reflected old colonial ways. Yet once, riding my bicycle, I passed him unnoticed in a crowded Cairo street. His face was ashen, averted, everted, and it wore an expression of such despair that I pressed down frantically on my pedals and fled.

Maître Prôst. I exchanged with him no more than a hundred words in a year. Thrice, he invited me—supreme accolade—to freely fence with him, man to man. I never saw anyone vanquish him on the *piste*.

On Paideia

True paideia is not only martial; it enables us to grow into (human) Being. Though they have become trite—*Musashi* now a bestseller in America—Zen and Bushido once offered a way of universal attentiveness, "not my song but yours," even as the sword flashes, timeless, to carve another's flesh out of time. But Bushido is irrecoverable to us in the West. What, then, in our schools, can quicken action, hone perception, calm the self—chattering macaque on a long leash—attune us to Being? What provisional silence can cleanse ideological discourse, dead speech?

To invoke such aims in our academies is to risk the charge of "mysticism." Mysticism: facile dismissal, favored by dogmatists intolerant of all but their narrow portion of reality. Was William James mystical? Proust, Einstein? Whence this academic hostility to mysticism, to its slightest aura or trace? A Marxist, Zionist, or feminist may prove no more rational than some "mystics," yet no stigma attaches itself to their commitment. Is it because men forgive attachments to factions, fractions— *my* side, *your* side—but never to the whole? The threat of mysticism: not vagueness or unreason, but a loyalty wider than most of us can bear. In short, Eros diffused, the Self dispersed, the end of paideia.

I was no mystic, nor could religion and athletics forever displace the erotic urgencies of my youth. But where, how, might such urgencies find clarity, let alone satisfaction, in Egypt?

My mother never spoke to me of sex. My father spoke only briefly, sometimes misleadingly, just enough to prevent older boys from "exploiting" me. No doubt, my defensive sexual education differed little from the kind young girls then received. Nor did any sex manuals contribute to my edification. The few Victorian tomes I discovered in our library menaced madness, blindness, venereal disease, not to mention Christian damnation, which held no terror for me. Much like other adolescents, everywhere, I pieced from my fantasies the realities of sex.

Servant girls were sometimes obliging; one pudgy maid, smiling pruriently, tried to seduce me when I was barely twelve. But their predatory hands and knowing airs repelled me; or else my own ineptitude stood in the way. Like Joseph Andrews, I remained chaste. What other recourse? Fear and pride precluded the services of prostitutes, shyness the society of *efrangeyas* (foreign girls). And it would have been dishonorable to "defile" a nubile girl of my milieu, over whom parents watched, in any case, with argus sight. What recourse then? An older woman, perhaps a widowed aunt, the kind one might meet in a novel by Colette? The closest I ever came to that phantasm was in Tante Alice.

Sensing my invincible shyness, my maternal uncles, inveterate womanizers, twitted me about my looks, my long lashes, my "way with the ladies"; their eyes danced wickedly, their heads bobbed, as I blushed and frowned. All teased me except my Uncle Ibrahim and his wife Alice. She was a long-legged Norman, hair pinned high in a russet bun. Thin veins, delicate like the pattern on a butterfly, sometimes showed in her cheeks. Her serious eyes rested on me as she spoke of the French Resistance, later of Sartre and Camus. When she carefully crossed her legs, I felt the rush of blood and wondered if my hair was not becoming ruddier than her own. Somehow, an alliance sprang between us—"we are different from the rest, aren't we?"—and remained tacit, erotic only by veiled, obscure implication.

My cousin, Hedayah tried to provoke me as Tante Alice never did. Two years older than I, Hedayah had handsome eyes, a pouty lower lip, and a tongue too tart for my taste. She would sit across from me, carefully exposing part of her thigh, then catching her young sister's warning glance, would shrug and in a stage whisper say: *"Mais il n'y a personne ici."* I would leave the room, affecting nonchalance, sensing Hedayah's yellow smile burn slowly in my back. Silently, I cursed in the same breath my lust, timidity, and shame.

Yet when I see today some boys and girls touch one another casually, as if zombies hid behind their lids, I am grateful for that intense constraint which gave my temper its tilt. Seeing a woman walk ahead of me down a Cairo street shaded by eucalyptus trees, hips swaying to the rhythm of her high heels, hair tossing, I would try compulsively to fix her fleeting figure in my mind, and invent for her a voice, a name, a face. Fancy-bred, clad in romance, such images could wrack me more than any naked expressions of desire.

The first romance of my youth took place by the sea, in a summer camp pitched among the dunes of Ras-el-barr, where the Nile meets the Mediterranean, far from any city or tree. She was a sun-goldened, green-eyed Jewess, whose name I never knew. She belonged to another camp, young men and women preparing to settle in Israel after the war. At night, under an immense, star-scattered sky, their songs rose above the rumbling surf, strange, alluring, to my ears. She did not surface like Cyprian Aphrodite from the foam; she first came into view riding a donkey, her bare thighs clamped firmly on the beast, smiling with her eyes. We never spoke, we needed no speech. Whatever daring I showed, swimming far or jumping high, I showed to her tender amusement.

Once the two camps played volleyball, Moslem against Jew. I can not recall who lost or won; I recall only the sun-lit down on that girl's arms, the spryness in her eyes shifting suddenly into darker hues. I recall bare bodies in the sun, bright, breezy sea-scapes, white sand lighter than spray. And I remember an uglier shadow: the clumsy, homosexual advance of a teammate bent on breaking the spell of my summer romance.

MUNICH

Nothing that dulls our erotic being but blunts our common perception of things. Some places dampen our vibrancy; however genial or picturesque, they soon become for me desolate. But Sally and I feel the presence of desire in the air in Munich. My son, Geoffrey, concurs. They now speak of a *Fräuleinwunder* as they once did of a *Wirtschaftswunder* in postwar Germany. At a Fasching Ball, we see what they mean: figures svelte yet full; thick cascading hair, auburn or gold; taut, glistening skin, bronzed in some exotic clime; high cheekbones and kirghiz eyes, evoking the steppes; generous mouths, teeth large and regular; bodies swaying tirelessly to music. These German women emanate a sensuality that nearly overwhelms. I observe, trying to inscribe each image in my memory, knowing well that it will soon fade. But I look almost dispassionately, delighting in the objective existence of each beauty, remembering that my father did the same—yes, till he died in his eighties, so my son, who saw his grandfather last in Cairo, claims.

I look then at Sally in her clarity, beauty. Suddenly, a jarring memory intervenes. I think of Brita, a slow, Swedish girl I met in Munich in 1959. With her began the first adultery of my former marriage, began my most wretched years. Is that why I have returned to Munich, to heal some old wound, which only Sally can heal? "I carry no wounds," I assure myself—and see my first, now dead, wife, Bolly, smile in her enigmatic way.

Again the Fasching Ball. The dance of desire has become a little frayed. Tonight, the last of Fasching, tomorrow, Ash Wednesday. After Dionysos, Christ.

Nothing seems to me now more preposterous than the strut of sex in Egypt. Young dandies picked their way gingerly through a society cluttered equally by cosmopolitan manners and old-fashioned, native constraints, only to slip on their own vanity as if on invisible banana peels.

I do not know how girls endured the farces of courtship. My female relatives whispered and giggled much of the day, wrote one another "discreet" notes, like characters in a play by Feydeau or Beaumarchais, and wisely kept their amorous secrets from young men my age. Secrets? Once my Uncle Mahmoud took me aside and whispered with mock-earnestness in my ear: "Ihab, the secret about women is that they have absolutely no secrets," then exploded in cynical laughter. But I was never cynical. I associated with my female cousins—Sanak and Amira, Hoda and Esmat, Hedayah and Amina—small subtle epiphanies, the aura of estrus and jasmine water, sounds of quick laughter hushed in over-furnished rooms. Above all, I imagined them bound to one another in a silken sorority, ambiguously benign, wholly exclusive.

Like most young Egyptian men those days, I had no girl friends. I attended fashionable cinemas—the Royal, the Roxy, the Palace, the Metropole—less to see the film than the girls in the audience, or rather, to be seen by them. On such solemn occasions, I shaved meticulously my sparse, pubescent beard, slapped quantities of Coty brilliantine on my hair, parting it on the left and combing it back, adjusted my starched, separable collar, tightened my tie to an impeccable knot, donned my gray, double-breasted pinstripe suit, and stepped out in shiny black shoes as if I had a tryst with Ava Gardner or Hedy Lamar.

Matinees were unfashionable; they drew only naïves who wanted to watch the film. Soirees, especially of American musicals, attracted a showy crowd. I arrived a little early to note which girls sat with their families in *loges* (boxes). During intermission, between the war newsreels and *le grand film,* I paced the aisles with a friend, then took a position in a conspicuous corner of the lobby, puffing on Camels or Lucky Strikes. Since I did not inhale, I flourished my cigarette, looked about a good deal, unsmiling, my center nowhere, my circumference everywhere.

None mistook me, though, for a true Cairo gallant. These older swells booked their seats in the first row of the mezzanine, arrived a few minutes late, and waited impatiently for the usher's flashlight to point their alligator shoes to their seats. During intermission, they flitted about, visiting friends in their *loges,* displaying golden rings, cufflinks, lighters, and cigarette cases on which they tapped their cigarettes for an unconscionable time before igniting them in a great puff of smoke. Afterwards, they drove off in their convertibles to Groppi's where, over a whisky or cassata, they debated women's legs: Ann Miller's, Ginger Rogers', Betty Grable's. Later still, they gambled at the Royal Automobile Club or met their mistresses, some ample Greek or Italian dancer, for whom they had rented a quiet *garçonnière*. The next day, they rose in time for lunch and kept inordinately busy, in clubs or cafés, "making important connections." Unerringly, their conversation turned to sex and money, about which they divagated in witty, obscene, and exhausting detail. Their paths crossed briefly mine. But their paths finally led deep into the rank corruption of Egypt, which I abhorred. In any event, I could not afford their company: my allowance for a year would not sustain them for a day. Thus I swung from one extreme to another as only adolescents swing. Now I dressed elegantly; now I contemned all outward show, but wanted that contempt to show. I dressed like a dandy less to please others than to distance, even alienate—and so re-create?—myself, as dandies since Brummel and Baudelaire have intuitively known. Then, estranged, I turned to the company of our cook, chauffeur, or butler, as I once did in childhood, though few now remained in our strained household for long.

I recall a particular summer evening with our cook, Suleyman. My parents had just left for Alexandria. As I chatted with Suleyman at dinner—he now both cooked and served my solitary meals—I discovered that he had never been to a movie. I took him to La Potinière, an outdoor cinema, to see "King Kong." We sat in straw armchairs on a terrace lined with potted geraniums and palms, waiting for the sky to darken, the performance to begin. In the twilight, Suleyman mused about his betrothed. "Some day, soon now, very soon, we'll get married," he said. "I will bring her from the village, and we'll settle *fi Masr* (in Cairo), *ya sidi*." Then the film started. Before long, the great, wondrous beast roared and lumbered into the audience; Faye Wray rolled her eyes and shrieked. Child-like, Suleyman gripped my arm, his face twitching, changing with every scene. At the end, his nimble black eyes were wet.

We strolled home, passing vendors of fresh corn on the cob, grilled aromatically on stoves hammered from old tin cans. I bought two, wrapped in their green sheaves to keep them warm. We munched silently; afterwards, Suleyman wiped his mouth primly on the sleeve of his *gallabiah.* When we reached home, Suleyman thanked me with dignity. Then, eyes moistening again: "You know, *ya sidi,* that poor old monkey, it's me, only bigger, much bigger. They killed him, he had nowhere to go in the city." A pause: "Are all movies sad like that?"

ON BEAUTY AND THE BEAST

What does the beast seek? Raw, unfinished, contingent, it finds in beauty completeness, inviolable repose. Yet beauty lacks the imaginative energy of the beast, its violence of delight as well as need.

Nature knows that desire requires display. The lion, the peacock, the praying mantis each follows its preordained part in the show. But the human creature is gaudier on nature's stage; the thespian arts have been bred in the genes.

All men have played the beast, pursued loveliness, lost in a crowd this Helen's or that Nefertiti's face, and losing it recovered desire once again. In such futile pursuits we regenerate the universe.

Once, on the Saw Mill River Parkway, I passed a woman driving a blue roadster, and catching a glimpse of her dazzling face, slammed on my brakes in sudden pain. I followed her car for an hour, through autumnal country lanes, till she vanished into a great, high-gated house. Was her beauty, then, all of my making, a feint of evolution meant to enliven this planet among the empty stars? Or is there a greed of the eye—say Rembrandt's inward gaze, consumed in its self-representations, or Ahab's baleful stare, striking through the mask—a greed that wants to grasp the very heart of things?

Plato thought Beauty was but the soul's memory of some vanished harmony or perfection waiting upon our re-cognition, an attribute of half-forgotten Being. That memory drives us still to reconstitute life in ever higher forms. We know it as desire. It inspires the Beast.

◆

False urgencies of spirit, sports, sex. They all had their shapes of excess as of ascesis, but they led me nowhere. By my second year at the university, I realized that rigor must become practical, generous—or else it stunts. I turned to work, sensing that my Great Escape from Egypt depended on professional achievement more than on existential quests. If I graduated with distinction, the Ministry of Education might award me a fellowship to study abroad.

At eighteen, I began to reproach myself for all the time I lost in erotic fantasies, time canceled in the onanistic fastness of movie houses, where I sat sometimes from noon to midnight. "You will never become a scientist or engineer that way," I admonished myself at least once a day. Then I would rush to my bicycle and race to the Faculty of Engineering, barely a mile away in Giza.

The University of Cairo, then, was a conglomerate of florid governmental buildings designed only for instruction; no student unions, cafeterias, or dorms obtained.

Unapproachable professors declaimed from the podium; assistants supervised anxious students in the labs; annual examinations determined the issue. No electives, no general education, no extracurricular activities except half a dozen sports. One matriculated in a particular branch of engineering—electrical, mechanical, civil, chemical—and learned nothing besides. Such illiberal education, though exigent, deterred creativity, blunted any ethical stance. Nor did it foster a sense of community within the various faculties of the university.

Indeed, the notorious student riots of Egypt may have been sparked less by political events than the need of fervent youths to meet one another in common hope. I recall vividly the time we occupied the Great Amphitheatre of the Faculty of Engineering, though I recall nothing of the grievance which drove us to strike. We barricaded ourselves for two days and two nights in that dim, cavernous place, subsisting on passion, candy, and rusty tapwater. At first, we made grandiloquent speeches, heartily applauding one another. Then, as heartily, we conducted "political workshops" whose true theme was our own intransigence. (In these, I tended to play Danton more than Robespierre.) Afterwards, we smoked, gossiped about god and eternity, while the more serious among us burrowed into their engineering textbooks. Exhausted at last, we tried to sleep on the hard, curved benches of the amphitheatre, jackets rolled beneath our heads, smelly socks in each other's noses. And we awoke, parched, red-eyed, and ravenous to repeat the day before.

Our families fretted; the deans chafed; *el bolice* lolled outside, yawning beneath their steel helmets. They could have flushed us out easily with their cudgels and canes;

but too many students there came from "good families,"
and the governor of Giza counseled restraint. Time took
their side, entropy ours. They made a few "concessions,"
rescinded them quietly later. We came out on the third
day, claiming *nasr* (victory).

Was it all futile bravado? Keen, restive, opinionated,
and if not incorruptible yet uncorrupted, Egyptian students still acted as the political and moral conscience of
the nation, as a mercurial index of its discontents. Some
of them, warped, intense spirits, felt their way gloomily
in the world; others squandered themselves in ribaldry.
Yet most joined in a camaraderie where loyalty took root,
friendship flowered naturally, and generosity flourished
even amid prickly rivalries.

Despite its dreary routines, the university could not
deaden us. At times, the drudgery of study gave way to
lambent visions, and the future danced like an incan-
descent genie caught in a will of fire. Blazing with a
knowledge we did not really possess, we dedicated ourselves to vast schemes: a new Moslem Empire, extending
from the English Channel to the China Sea; or a rebirth
of the ancient gods, Amon, Isis, Osiris and Set, to sup-
plant the barbarism of Islam and usher in new mysteries;
or a concept of Universal Justice, reinstating the fellah
and reapportioning the land without spilling blood; or,
again, some miraculous, technological plan to turn all
the deserts of North Africa into a green paradise—and
always, of course, the expulsion of the British from Egypt.
Such were the reciprocities of history and dream, the
overweening desires of youths at once too young and
old for their years.

The friends I made in that flush of manhood gave me
the formative experience of friendship itself though all

have now disappeared from my life. Talat, Riyad, Michel, my fencing mates—of course, they called us the Four Musketeers! Talat, fiery, pinch-faced, persecuted me earlier at Saidiah till I learned to lash out like him, arms flailing and feet kicking the air. He returned to befriend me through our university years, and later at the University of Pennsylvania where we both earned our doctorates. Gentle Riaz, Francophone and Francophile, could barely speak Arabic when we met. "May I sit with you in the same drawer?" he asked me on our first day at the Faculty of Engineering, proposing to share a locker for our drafting instruments. He, too, came to America and took his graduate degree at MIT. As for Michel, lank, languid, yet in a race fleet as an ostrich, with droopy, half-cynical eyelids belying his artistic temper, he became a gifted architect.

But where are they now? And the others: Elie, Fawzy, Ibrahim, Roshdy, Hamed, those bright, best friends of my class? Where? Perhaps it is in the nature of friendship that it possesses the wisdom to lapse, though in our youth we would have vehemently denied this, sure of time and our own hearts.

———◆———

In the middle of my five-year university course, something inexplicable happened: *I failed a subject.*

I stood in front of the Faculty Bulletin Board. Hundreds of students pressed, squirmed, shoved, to catch a glimpse of their names among those who had passed the year's examinations. Some friends looked at me silently as they left. I stood there like a broken column, and still stood in the empty hall, long after everyone left, staring at the board which denied my name.

———◆———

INTERLUDE

Autobiographer: The facts are simple. You failed me-
chanics at the end of your third year.
You had the summer to prepare for
the make-up examination. You passed.
Why this gloom?
I.H.: (Silence)
Autobiographer: You lost no time, only face.
I.H.: I lost self-esteem. I was in self-mourn-
ing. I lay in bed, as if encased in lead,
aching within. Only study relieved that
internal wound.
Autobiographer: The wound of pride, egotism?
I.H.: (Silence)
Autobiographer: But why did you fail in the first place?
I.H.: Improvidence of feeling, imprecision
of thought. I was too needy, greedy.
My mind went soft with self- concern.

◆

As I approached graduation, the war neared its end.
Most Egyptians, of course, considered the war merely
as a struggle between factions of European colonialism;
D-Day meant less to them than El Alamein. British soldiers, and even the rambunctious "Aussies," went now
unnoticed on the streets. But American GIs, who appeared increasingly on Cairo streets, met with curiosity,
good will. *El Yankees*, after all, had never occupied Egyptian soil, and they brought a history known better for
its idealism than imperialism. (Now, alas, we know these
to be all too compatible.) They arrived, as well, after a
million Hollywood myths had long invaded our heads.

For me, the termination of the war meant one thing only: I could sail to America. Throughout the war, I was as little affected by it as I had been by *la Crise* (the Depression) a decade earlier. To be sure, sandbags and anti-aircraft emplacements appeared at various public sites—ministries, bridges, powerhouses, waterworks. And on the flat roof of our house, near El Gala Bridge, a Lewis machine-gun stood idle except when I would persuade two slack Egyptian Army soldiers to let me scan the empty horizon in its sights. For a year or so, a blackout seemed sporadically in effect. We all lined our curtains, painted our window panes black, and forgot to close them at night. Once or twice, the air raid sirens shrieked. We would rush to our balconies or into the streets, pointing excitedly at the long, luminous beams sweeping the sky. Then someone would murmur: "Oh, it must have been a stray *Italiani* plane." And everyone would laugh.

What, then did the war mean to Cairenes? Distant slaughter; armies hurtling back and forth across school maps; headlines growing larger; loud Movietone newsreels on every screen; the streets full of alien soldiers, escorting more *efrangeyas* than we thought Egypt held; English speech pouring everywhere into our ears, displacing French as the foreign tongue; hotels, restaurants, cafés, movie houses, shops, alive with money and bought sex; native officials, contractors, profiteers growing suddenly rich; involuted arguments about the war, who will win, and what Egypt stood to gain or lose; above all, a sense of expectancy, waiting not so much for the end of the war itself as for a new order, a post-colonial dispensation—and, for me, the start of another life.

In the countryside, fellahs continued to draw water

from the Nile with their *sakiah, shadoof, tambour.* In the provincial cafés, *el kary* recited in sing-song the Koran, and old storytellers recounted the epic of Abu Zayed El Hilali, killed at last by a blind enemy who aimed his poisoned arrow by the great sound of the hero's urination. ("Allah," Abu Zayed cried, "you have only punctured my water gourd," whereupon the enemy fell dead of fright.) And in the desert, the bedouins maintained their ancient feuds, burying each other alive in the sand—or burying their children only to the neck as a cure against rheumatism.

Of the war's enormity, of its carnage and waste, few Egyptians had any sense till the very end, when images of Dachau and Auschwitz, Dresden and Hiroshima, began to appear in newspapers and on movie screens. Were Egyptians, then, like so many children at a historical play, cheering a spectacle they thought to leave behind when the final curtain fell? Did *I* look upon the Second World War with the same eyes, fantasy-glazed, that once dwelled on pictures of Big Bertha and the Red Baron's Fokker, in the *London Illustrated Gazette,* as if they were big toys?

———————◆———————

In the last two years at the university, I consecrated myself to work, schooldays and holidays, mornings, afternoons, nights. To my distress, I discovered that my mind had become lax, my calculations careless, my solutions slapdash. I set about to reverse this trend, practicing logarithms at dawn till I could feel my brain purr like a balanced, well-oiled rotor.

I specialized in electrical engineering, which carried a certain cachet—long before Marshall McLuhan, Egyptians considered electronics the science of the new day.

But I preferred theoretical questions, solved elegant problems with gaiety. I found tinkering in labs tedious, and thought tools and instruments malevolent, or at least obdurate in a peculiarly mindless way. (I was never a collector—stamps, shells, coins, guns—favoring existential flow, feeling, perception, over the collocation of objects in a dead space.) Like Henry Adams, I saw electricity as force, a force, though, closer to the unnameable power of Allah or Jahweh than to the mediate glory of the Virgin.

Aniconic in temper, I still missed in my engineering studies the human presence, its pathos, its sensuous, imaginative, wounded power. Lines, numbers, tables, ratios everywhere—but unless we can learn to sing like "golden-thighed Pythagoras" (Yeats), or like Euclid can "Look upon Beauty bare" (Millay), surely the soul must slowly wither. So I thought, looking askance at my companions fidgeting with their vacuum tubes, capacitors, and rheostats.

Sometimes, on weekends, I would snatch a day or two to read poetry or fiction. Locked up in my stale study, cross-legged in an old black leather armchair, I read for fifteen hours at a stretch, until my mother protested outside my door. I read first in the morocco-bound, gilded sets in my father's library: Corneille, Conrad, Scott, Flaubert, Thiers, Goethe, Macaulay, Dickens, Shakespeare, Gibbon, Jules Verne, books acquired long before by someone concerned with their decorative effect. Then I began to frequent the lending library of the British Council, near *Midan el Opera*. Housed in a clean, bright basement, with direct access to the street, the library smelled of unopened books, binding glue, glossy paper, and the fresh fragrance of its comely young English librarian. Still shy, I rarely spoke to her except to say "Hello" and "Thank you," though I remained conscious of her presence even as I leafed through novels on the "adventure" shelves: Charles Read, Rudyard Kipling, Charles Kingsley, Robert Louis Stevenson, W. H. Hudson, Frederick Marryat, Somerset Maugham.

The works that stormed my imagination then—like Maugham's *The Moon and Sixpence* and *The Razor's Edge*—might go begging for a place in the high canon of fiction today; but they were the works I needed, somehow, to release some inchoate idea of myself, some obscure promise. I read, at any rate, with headlong absorption, a mood that I envy now as I approach "serious literature"—let alone poststructuralist criticism—with mind frowning and pencil in hand.

After each reading orgy, bitter self-reproof. Electronics, not literature, will bring my release, I argued; once out of Egypt, I could read what I willed. I returned to my work with the single-mindedness of the Count of Monte Cristo plotting his escape from Chateau d'If. I passed my fourth year exams with the grade of "Good." I resolved to graduate in my fifth year with "Distinction." My parents now receded from my horizon; so did my spiritual quests, athletic feats, erotic reveries. I spoke only to my closest friends, spoke to them only of gausses, volts, amperes. When the phone rang for me, it was Riaz, Talat, or Ibrahim checking the solution to a problem in calculus or circuitry. I went to bed, after midnight, my head humming with numbers till I fell in Newton's sleep.

Yet a moment came in that last febrile year which offered brief relief—and prefigured my enduring passion for travel. In their graduating year, students could take an optional trip, traveling south to Aswan then north to Alexandria to inspect electric installations from one end of Egypt to the other. The few who could afford the expense went eagerly, excitedly, less to see generators, transformers, radio transmitters, hydroelectric stations, than to obey the call of high adventure—or at least low romance.

Oddly enough, I can remember only the texture of time on that trip, only a few entranced scenes. I recollect the long, sleepless train ride south, with a stop at Luxor, where I spent a late afternoon walking alone through the Temple of Karnak. The power of columnar stone and emblematic history wrapped itself around me there as I wandered at sundown, the last light mingling with tinctures of eternity, my spirit awed, oppressed, struggling to come free. I recall, too, a *felucca* ride on the Nile, after a torrid day at the Old Aswan Dam, my fellow engineers, mouths smeared with mango juice, singing bawdy songs while the *rais* roared nautical orders between refrains as we passed the craggy island of Elephantine. In Alexandria, I see another scene: a flock of lavendered girls chattering in some foreign tongue, then darting into a pastry shop, pointing and laughing as they choose their *éclairs* or *mille-feuilles*. I tarry outside the half-glazed pane, watching their quick shadows, the smell of lavender and burnt sugar in my nose. Alexandria again: I stand with Riaz on our balcony at the Cecil Hotel, high above the crowded seaside *corniche*, counting and re-counting on the horizon every trace of smoke, every speck of sail, the water sparkling like fire-opal. "What ship shall carry us farther than eye can see?"

When I returned to Cairo after a fortnight, I realized calmly, though that calmness itself hurt, that I had missed no one, no one at all. I had not been born, it seems, to miss my home.

On Travel

What brings on the traveling mood? Though it is not always metaphysical like Ishmael's ("Whenever I find myself growing grim about the mouth; whenever it is a damp, drizzly November in my soul; whenever I find myself involuntarily pausing before coffin warehouses, and bringing up the rear of every funeral I meet . . .— then, I account it high time to get to sea as soon as I can."), that mood moves us all.

I know counselors against travel. Thoreau boasted that he "traveled much in Concord"; and Emerson said, "We owe to our first journeys the discovery that place is nothing. . . . My giant goes with me wherever I go." True, travel may betray some insufficiency in us, a dubious need that deeper natures refuse. Still, the Koran says: "And God hath spread the earth as a carpet for you, that ye may walk therein through spacious paths." Walking these paths, we learn the ways of men, and meet in ourselves the stranger we most dread to meet. We experience the world interactively, feeling the shock of differences even as we absorb them in us. Seeing how human beings vary in shape, language, custom, creed, can we hope to coax our distinctions into wider civility?

But voyages are also errancies of the soul; they whisper of the unknown. Who has not turned the corner of a strange street and come suddenly upon Gautama, Cleopatra, Tamburlaine? Voyages whisper loss, departure, things thrown to the wind, and evoke that very country "from whose bourne no traveler ever returns." In journeys, we hear the cadences of the universe itself, and endure our death, going hence, coming hither. "Ripeness is all." As I write this, aged fifty-five, in a foreign city, I wonder about my traveling mood, if I could leave all my friends, belongings, books, all familiar faces and places, back in Milwaukee, never to return, as I never returned to Cairo.

I graduated in June 1946 from the Faculty of Engineering, second in my class. A Catholic, Elie Aziz, placed first; two Copts, Faiz and Ibrahim, came third and sixth; and my two close friends, Talat and Riaz, ranked fourth and fifth. All six, in a class of more than a hundred graduates, received "Distinction." The Ministry of Education awarded Talat, Riaz, and me—nominal Moslems—opulent fellowships to study electronics abroad. A year later, the ministry offered similar fellowships to the three Christians.

But where should I go? England, Switzerland, America? No one in my family favored England. My mother, of course, preferred Switzerland; it was "closest, and very scenic besides." My father, though reluctant to see his son leave, argued forcefully for America. Its technology was peerless then; it held the future in its keep. As for myself, I was implacably set on studying in the United States—and set secretly on remaining there. My father and I prevailed, first over my mother, then over the Ministry of Education itself, which reserved its choice, expensive "missions" to America for graduates with political clout.

I still faced frightening medical and bureaucratic ordeals. To secure my "educational mission" and my student visa to the United States, I had to prove my health, sanity, financial responsibility, and impeccable moral character. I had to prove acceptance at a reputable American university. And I had to obtain trans-Atlantic passage at a time when returning GIs preempted both shipping berths and college admissions. But having come so close to my goal, I had no intention of faltering.

Predictably, I found the medical inquisition the worst. (To this day I avoid doctors, visit them only when I am in the best of health.) Teams of Egyptian physicians (rather crude), then American specialists (somewhat cool), examined me for everything, trachoma, *bilharzia*, tuberculosis, all rampant in Egypt, for every trace of mental or physical degeneracy. For the first time in my life, someone prodded my anus, pulled painfully on my testicles; another searched my arms with a needle for a vein, almost without success; still another pounded my chest and kidneys as if practicing on a drum; yet another peered down my throat till I gagged. Blood, urine, feces, spittle were extracted from my body. Then they sent me home, with many a dark look, to await the results. These took an interminable month, my humor swinging wildly from anxiety to hope, hope to despair, despair to anxiety again. Finally, the reports came, pronouncing me fit except for some small excess of albumin, which our family doctor cured with injections and pills and the recommendation to eat a great deal of watermelon that summer.

My interview with the American consul, a brisk, crew-cut Stanford man, proved more civilized. Behind rimless glasses, he quickly ascertained that I could speak English, appeared sane enough, had not practiced pimping or prostitution, and felt no sympathy for communism. The medical reports, the police record (blank), the Egyptian Educational Mission Award, all lay on his desk; so did a letter of admission from the Moore School of Electrical Engineering of the University of Pennsylvania. The consul did not press the point about the missing trans-Atlantic ticket, having been assured by our family friend, Colonel Siemen, that he would help secure my passage. In my immaculate new passport, the consul placed a student visa, stamped with the Great Seal of the United States of America, and, with a combined shove and handshake, showed me to the next room. There, a burly U.S. Marine forcefully fingerprinted both my hands, gave me a large slab of Palmolive and a clean linen towel, and pointed silently to the wash bowl.

Colonel Siemen called a week later to say that my passage to America had been arranged on the S. S. *Abraham Lincoln,* leaving from Port Said in late August. He had written earlier to recommend me to the University of Pennsylvania, his alma mater. I do not know what prompted his improbable friendship with my parents. They met at some reception in the flush of the Allied victory, and in the untrammeled feeling of the day found in each other some baffling affinity. He introduced himself affably as judge advocate in the U.S. Army, an American Jew. Around his round, blue eyes he wore a round, gold pince-nez, and wore over his small, pear-shaped body baggy uniforms. His preternatural quickness of mind, of intuition really, seemed always generous; his gaze penetrated everyone even as it promised sympathy. I shall never know why he liked me; I know only that his intercessions proved decisive in my life.

In that hot, fateful summer of 1946, as I desperately waited for all the pieces of my life to fit, I walked one still evening across Kasr-el-Nil Bridge—now renamed Tahrir (Liberation)—alone, sick at heart, and sick in the stomach of those albumin pills. I had not eaten; my mouth was parched; the bridge seemed to stretch without end beneath my leaden feet. In my eyes, the lamplight shone yellow, bleary, washing down like fluid rust on the iron railings. I felt congested, clotted, like some lump of clay yearning to lose its shape in the earth. Yet there was a tightness in my mind, an edge of resolve somewhere, that would not obey the call of dust. I thought to myself: why, this must be despair—despair checked by some deeper trust.

4

Passages: 1946–1985

I DISCOVERED AMERICA on a Liberty Ship, which had barely survived the war, lurching toward New York on its last voyage. The ship creaked continually, and left in the ocean a wake of rust. During the passage, a longshoreman's strike closed the Port of New York, forcing "Old Abe" to veer south toward New Orleans. The voyage stretched; the empty days came and went, invariable. I could fill them only with anticipation. But my severance from everything familiar, from the very languages that housed my feelings, heightened my anxieties, my senses. Sea-smells everywhere—spume, fried fish, capstan grease, oily soot floating from the single smokestack. At night, I dreamed exorbitantly. My fellow passengers—some military derelicts, a few on sick leave, a few nondescript civilians, all Americans somehow uneager to reach any port—seemed to me phantasms.

At last, one morning, the ship rounded Key West. A long night after, it began to glide through the Mississippi Delta. As a schoolchild, I had learned that the Nile was the longest, the stateliest river, the great artery of history; it flowed like "some grave mighty thought threading a dream" (Leigh Hunt). The Mississippi ranked only third in length. Yet sliding through the bayou in that strange dawn, the air thick, the horizon still clotted with darkness, I sensed hidden luxuriance and menace. Everywhere, a nameless vegetation threatened to clog the channels and ensnare the ship which slipped through like a huge sea snail. The air was humid as I had never known it in Egypt, the sky low. I had not sailed farther up the Nile than Abu Simbel, and so never felt the wild pulse of Africa. Yet knowing Conrad, I now imagined myself, like Marlowe, pushing into the heart of darkness. Blacks began to appear in curious skiffs around Old Abe. And how odd! These blacks spoke English, a kind of English, wore European trousers, shirts, hats.

I had entered America, it seemed, from its secret, gloomy underside, not like Columbus or "stout Cortez." Yes, I had read the boys' books, *Deerslayer, Tom Sawyer, Atala,* but had never really believed that modern America could be anything but a romance of Europe, El Dorado civilized. I felt now, exhilaration contending with dread, that I had come to a land more extravagant than any of my recent dreams. A country younger than Egypt but also older, claiming the precedence of a primeval jungle over the most archaic temple. Here I was on my own at last. But what awaited me at the end of this swampy river? Liberty—or some immane power, without bounds or name?

◆

Forty years have passed. I have changed countries, careers, marriages. I have traveled three times around the earth. But I have never returned to Egypt, though Geoffrey Karim Hassan—Jeff to his friends, Karim to his grandparents, to his parents Geoffrey—has visited Egypt twice in the intervening decades. The country he saw is one I know and do not know:

—Geofffrey like me has climbed the Great Pyramid and wandered through its labyrinths alone. (He likes narrow places; I don't.) He drove out there with his mother on a road cluttered with shacks, factories, high-rise suburbs. When I drove out with my parents, to take tea at the Mena House, I saw only rice fields as far as the eye could see.

—He has dined with my parents at the exclusive Gezira Sporting Club, and heard them complain about its "decline" since the early postwar years. I could never have set foot there, nor could they: in prewar days, it was a purely British preserve.

—He has ridden with his mother on a train to Aswan: "You should see those trains, people climbing out of windows, riding on top of carriages, carrying animals and poultry in cages. Unbelievable! We looked at each other, and I said: 'Oh, boy.' Then we found our first-class compartment. Wonderful pictures on the walls, bucket seats, air conditioning. And only army officers. We sat next to this Egyptian Army officer, he must have weighed three hundred pounds." In my days: no army officers, except a general, perhaps, could have afforded first class. No air conditioning or bucket seats.

—He has journeyed by bus from Alexandria to Cairo: "Lots of military jeeps everywhere. Lots of signs saying 'Forbidden This, Forbidden That.' But as soon as you enter Cairo, everything is open, free. A taxi drives into the side of the tourist bus, then backs off honking. The bus driver doesn't even look. The street's so crowded, the same taxi runs into the side of the bus again. The tourists can't believe it. The bus driver mops his brow, doesn't look." It is true, then, what I read, that Cairo has become a city of dense smog, traffic snarls, skiff-dwellers, collapsing buildings, immense garbage dumps, raw sewage overflowing the streets?

—He has met his grandparents: "The first time I went to Egypt, your father was still alive. He was really sharp. Your mother let him organize everything. But the second time, he had already died, and your mother was kind of vague. Uncle Osama brought her in his Mercedes to the airport to greet us, and she hardly recognized my mother or me." I try to imagine my parents in their advanced years, and how many times their marital relations changed, reversed like an hourglass by their own inexorable needs.

—Geoffrey has met the "other Ihab." Ihab's parents, the Salehs, cater to my mother in her widowed old age. The Salehs fabricate wills, forge deeds, spread rumors, but keep my mother content in her forgetful and crotchety ways. Their stroke of genius: calling their now-six-year-old son Ihab—rare name in Egypt—to blend his image with mine. Later, my cousin Osama, a lawyer, untangles the legal web. I think to myself: "Nothing there has really changed."

◆

I complete—complete?—this autobiography in Milwaukee, where I live and teach, now home. I like this spacious Midwestern city, except in the reluctant spring. I like its candid cityscape, spare population, fitful lake, forever changing colors from tan to blue-green through a spectrum of fluid shades. I like even its cold climate—let others seek the Sun Belt.

But why this autobiography now? What's this that has come late to roil my life, stirring impure memories, as if to prove Wordsworth right, that "the child is father of the man"? Yes, Memory is sister to Poesy, poorer sister clad in gray garb of recall. And Poesy is what I adored—next to Spirit—when I was young. Or is autobiography my own warrant for American self-exile?

Men and women have flocked to America, fleeing or seeking, driven by the most diverse motives. But the psychological exile stands apart, his case shadier, thicker with complicity and silent intrigue. Who are these beings, full of dark conceits, rushing to meet the future while part of them still stumbles about, like a blind speleologist, in caverns of the past? What urgency speaks through their self-banishment?

All leaving is loss, every departure a small death—yes, journeys secretly know their end. Yet self-exile may also conceal a deeper exigency. Thus Rilke's Malte Laurids Brigge:

It will be difficult to persuade me that the story of the Prodigal Son is not the legend of him who did not want to be loved. When he was a child, everybody in the house loved him. . . . But as a boy he sought to lay aside such habits.

And why should any boy, any man, nourish the "profound indifference of his heart," and so refuse love? Brigge proposes a harsh version of holiness:

What did they [family, friends, compatriots, comforters] know of him? He was now terribly difficult to love, and he felt that One alone was able for the task. But He was not yet willing.

This too is self-exile, prideful, it would seem, and contemptuous of the interdebtedness of all human hearts. Yet pride may also stand humbly at the door of sanctity. Isak Dinesen offers her version of pride, a different pride, pure and self-heedless:

Pride is faith in the idea that God had, when he made us. A proud man is conscious of the idea, and aspires to realize it. He does not strive toward a happiness, or comfort, which may be irrelevant to God's idea of him. His success is the idea of God, successfully carried through, and he is in love with his destiny.

What, then, had I really hoped to discover in America? It was not holiness: rather, scope, an openness of time, a more viable history. I also looked for some private space wherein to change, grow; for I had not liked what I foresaw of my life in Eternal Egypt. And so I left—no, fled—detesting all arguments from the blood and suspecting the force of my own detestation. Always, though, I sensed that something other, larger, than myself was at stake, as if my selfish hegira could still evoke a small, wry smile in heaven.

◆

Sometimes, sitting in Milwaukee on a moody afternoon, I try to imagine what my life in Egypt might have been. I cannot do it; an iron door clangs shut. But then, in our travels, passing through some distant, provincial town—Kwangju, Lublin, Djikili, Jinan, Tromsø—I have a sudden, dreadful intuition of what it must mean to exist there, from birth to death, feeling the blood, the years, leak away. I had a still nearer intuition of Egypt, passing through Athens some years ago: a stifling moment of heat, dust, noise, young men in short sleeves drifting through shabby streets, old ornate buildings, their cornices, caryatides, peeling on hovels below—most of all, the sense of durance, merciless contraction in the gut. It was, finally, an intuition of prisons: hospitals, asylums, monasteries, dungeons, any occluded relation or caved-in self.

Such places, though, may offer a supreme spiritual challenge. I first felt that challenge in Egypt when I thought that my plans for leaving might miscarry. I felt it again, decades later, reading Thomas Mann's *The Holy Sinner,* in which the incestuous saint, Pope Gregory, clings to a tiny, bare, rock island for seventeen years in harsh penance. Then, later still, I saw in London Arnold Wesker's play, *Caritas,* concerning Christine Carpenter, a fourteenth-century anchoress who renounced the world and immured herself in a vault not larger than a roomy grave. How can spirit subsist in such stony confinement, without day or night, unless it breaks out into vast inner spaces? Was it not precisely there, in that intolerable constriction of need, implosion of desire, that heroic destinies were clarified like diamonds in the burning, black bowels of the earth?

For a long time after leaving Egypt, I had a bad, recurrent dream. I dreamt that I was compelled to go back, complete some trivial task—close a door left ajar, feed a canary, whisper a message. There was terror in that banal dream, terror and necessity, and also the sense, within the dream itself, that I had dreamt it before, and within that a feeling that each time I dreamt the dream, something would work out: I would no longer need to go back. The dream became less frequent with the years, after Sally entered my life; to my conscious knowledge, I no longer dream it. Is that dreamlessness itself but subterfuge? I like to think of it, rather, as a hint of unconcern, that heedlessness or detachment which comes, to those who seek it, in good season.

Yet so long as Sally lives, I remain attached, heedful, worldly enough to fear, fight, delight—enough to love. And if Sally dies?

———————◆———————

I have experienced the pain of only one person's death, that of Bolly, my first wife.

When she and I were divorced, in the spring of 1966, I did not need to appear in the Middletown courthouse. But we went out afterwards, for a last dinner together, at a Connecticut River inn. Neither of us ate very much. We spoke a little of Geoffrey, of how he and Sally liked each other. Bolly wore a black silk dress with black mesh stockings. She died twelve years later:

I think back of a wintry day in Connecticut: deep snow, the woods stark, grey and white birches peeling against a ragged sky, the streams almost frozen, trickling blue-black beneath the ice. Dead of winter, they say, and I had come to visit a woman dying.

I brought a dozen perfect yellow roses from the airport. She protested the gift, pleased, while she put them in an earthen pot she had turned. She wanted to burden no one;

her self-pity, if any survived her convent childhood, remained invisible; over the years, her solitude became essential. We played a record I had also brought, sonatas for
violin and clavier, in the glassed-in parlor. The winter sun
filtered through the birches. I kept thinking: "Mozart and
terminal cancer in one room." She bragged shyly about her
"other" healthy organs. When she looked at the late light
on the snowdrift outside she said: "It's beautiful." I wondered: "What world she sees there with those slate-green
eyes?" Before I left, she gave me a sliced apple to "freshen
my mouth."

I would not go with her, though she asked me twice, to
a large Sunday brunch given by old friends in Middletown.

Ihab Hassan
The Right Promethean Fire

I write, I write even death. Yet in this fragmentary
autobiography so much eludes me—and so much I
must refuse to write.

Throughout my childhood, I saw in my father's study
a large picture of a famous Egyptian statue, *The Cross-
Legged Scribe* (c. 2500 B.C.). I viewed the picture with
vague distaste: something in the wide, staring eyes and
splotched limestone skin, in the sagging breasts and
passive, sedentary pose, repelled me. Decades later, I
saw the original in the Louvre, and have stood before
it, many times since, entranced.

New qualities have emerged from this piece of
wrought clay: sentience, alertness, skill. The large,
faun-like ears stick out, as if listening intently to every
voice, every trace of sense in the cosmic noise. A touch
asquint, the eyes look deeply in as well as out. The
thin mouth, high cheekbones, angular jaws, suggest a
focused will, pleasure in all things true and exact.

Long, shapely fingers, subtle in their authority, hint aesthetic refinement in a body perhaps too poised, too symmetrical, in its repose. I go away, each time, with the feeling that something unique was, still is, in this man's keeping: delight, mastery, a gnostic power that has chosen the lineaments of a scribe to speak across the ages. This squinting, squatting man, I think, lived under the sign of *Medu-netcher,* the Word, the Logos.

The Word has its holy and profane histories. From Paleolithic cave painting to hieroglyph, hieratic and demotic. The Phoenician alphabet, the Greek, the Roman. Irish Seminuncials, Alcuin's Caroline. Then Italian Cursive, German Gothic. Gutenberg, Caxton, Juan Pablos (first printer in the Americas) . . . McLuhan. And beyond McLuhan: electronic "painting," laser beams:

We have watched the alphabet evolve from prehistoric painting on the wall of a Spanish cave—discovered by a girl and brought to the attention of the world when she called to her father, "Toros! Toros!"—to the most intricate, most complicated, almost other-world developments of electronic letter-making.

Oscar Ogg
The 26 Letters

In Milwaukee, I envisage the *Cross-Legged Scribe* as I sit in my Scandinavian writing chair, pencil in hand. The Scribe knew all the Divine Words, and the sacred baboon and ibis of Thoth guarded his labors, and his spirit moved gracefully between the Kingdom of the Living and the Kingdom of the Dead. But I labor only with *medu,* the profane speech of men. I consult the *Oxford English Dictionary,* Webster's *Third New Inter-*

national, Roget's *Thesaurus.* I cannot read the old, mystic friezes, furiously defaced by Christians in Dendera, in all the awesome temples of Egypt; I cannot name the Pharaohs since Menes, Narmer, Khasekhemui, and Djoser; I have no reckoning of granaries or floods, wars or stars, of slaves, priests, masons, or charioteers. I do not even know all the gods. I simply "write"— without foreknowledge or primal recall.

———◆———

Do you not know, O Asclepius, that Egypt is the copy of Heaven, or rather, the place where here below are mediated and projected all operations which govern and actuate the heavenly forces? Even more than that, if the whole truth is to be told, our land is the temple of the entire World. Nevertheless, since it is fitting that wise men should have foreknowledge of all things, you should not be unacquainted with this. There will be a time when it will be manifest that it was in vain that the Egyptians cherished godhead with pious will and constant devotion, and all holy reverence for the gods will vanish and be made of no effect. . . . Then this most holy land, the abode of shrines and temples, will be most full of graves and of dead men.

Hermes Trismegistus

———◆———

Some things have come to me like grace: Sally, a sane body, a few friends. Most things I strove to earn: America, and all that America has enabled in my life. But I am not certain that grace and effort are not tangents to our souls, tangents meeting every night in the dark.

When I think of the Egypt I fiercely fled, on which the sun rose in the clear, dry dawn of history and now has set, perhaps never to rise again; when I think of the America to which I deliriously came, a land violently dreaming the world into a better place; when I think of everything real, implacable in my existence, which neither age nor tragedy can dim—when I think of these, I know then that Time has kept its secret from my prying mind, and that all my writing, this autobiography, remains vain. But I know, too, with the deeper, stranger certainty of faith, that such "vanity" is itself augury and sign. We come to sentience in a universe where even our absurdities speak.

Out of Egypt, into middles, passages, falling into true time.

IHAB HASSAN, one of the world's leading critics of modern literature—and increasingly of postmodern consciousness in its many manifestations—left Cairo, Egypt, in 1946 to study engineering in the United States. Later becoming a naturalized U.S. citizen, Professor Hassan has had a distinguished teaching career at Rensselaer Polytechnic Institute, Weslyan University, and, currently, the University of Wisconsin–Milwaukee. Professor Hassan's early works *Radical Innocence* (1961), *The Literature of Silence* (1967), and *The Dismemberment of Orpheus* (1971) have become classics of modern literary criticism; his recent books include *Paracriticisms* (1975) and *The Right Promethean Fire* (1980), both of which show his widening interest in imagination, science, cultural change, and autobiography. His forthcoming books are *The Postmodern Turn,* his latest statement on the subject, and *Spirit of Quest,* which concerns spiritual adventure in contemporary American literature.